GO WILD

GO WILD

Text by Claire Berrisford

An Hachette UK Company
www.hachette.co.uk

Summersdale Publishers Ltd
Part of Octopus Publishing Group Limited
Carmelite House
50 Victoria Embankment
LONDON
EC4Y 0DZ
UK

www.summersdale.com

Printed and bound in China

ISBN: 978-1-78685-772-9

Substantial discounts on bulk quantities of Summersdale books are available to corporations, professional associations and other organisations. For details contact general enquiries: telephone: +44 (0) 1243 771107 or email: enquiries@summersdale.com.

Disclaimer: Neither the author nor the publisher can be held responsible for any loss or claim arising out of the use, or misuse, of the suggestions made herein.

GO WILD

FIND FREEDOM

AND

Adventure

IN THE

GREAT OUTDOORS

CHRIS NAYLOR

summersdale

CONTENTS

iNTRODUCTiON

>>>————————————————➤

Life in the modern age is demanding. Our minds and bodies can feel strained from the constant drive to do more, the pressure to achieve more and the compulsion to stay connected to the fast-paced, digital world. Bombarded by stimuli, we are pushing ourselves to our limits.

The simple fact is, we are not suited to an indoor life, spending hours hunched over screens. We are adapted to walk in green spaces, to run and swim and to explore; to live in harmony with nature – not separate from it. For thousands of years humans lived in the outdoors, so an affinity with nature is in our DNA. All we need to do is find our way back to it.

This book will help you reconnect with the great outdoors. It can be hard to get away, or to even know where to start, but whether you like to walk, run or swim, take part in sports, admire wildlife, or forage for wild foods, within these pages there will be something to inspire you to get out in the fresh air and reignite your sense of wonder at the natural world around you.

Nature is a balm for the body and the soul. Even just 30 minutes spent in a natural space can reduce blood pressure, improve concentration, give our mood a boost and nourish our sense of creativity. It's the salve that we need to heal our physical and mental well-being, and it's the key to our health and happiness.

So, as soon as you have the chance, escape to the great outdoors and embrace all the adventures it has to offer. Open your heart and mind to new experiences, seek out what inspires you and what scares you. Be curious, be bold, be filled with awe – and go wild!

WILDERNESS
IS NOT A
LUXURY
BUT A
NECESSITY
OF THE
HUMAN
SPIRIT.

EDWARD ABBEY

THE GREAT OUTDOORS

To help you feel at ease in the midst of nature and to make the most of what's around you, read on to discover the key bushcraft tips that every explorer should know. These skills will keep you safe and savvy in the outdoors and ensure that you have a trip to remember for many years to come.

THE GREAT OUTDOORS 101

>>>———————————————————▶

Whether you're going out for an afternoon walk in the fields close to home or planning an epic week-long trip in the mountains, there are some basic rules that you should always bear in mind.

Tell someone else: Always make sure someone else (outside of your party) knows where you're going and when you expect to return. If you're making good choices and taking the right precautions, it's unlikely that you will experience any problems. But nature is unpredictable and should the weather take an unexpected turn for the worse, or if you or one of your party incurs an injury partway through your trip, having someone on the outside who's able to check in with you or raise the alarm in an emergency is an extra safety net.

Get permission: Before heading out on a run, hike, swim or camping trip that will take you off designated trails and away from official sites, make sure you have permission from the landowner to be there, and that you're following any rules and regulations of the area.

Be prepared: Do your best to be prepared for any eventuality. Check the weather before you leave and pack accordingly: bring water, a first-aid kit, a map and a method of communication, whether it's a phone or Satellite Emergency Notification Device (SEND). Although the latter is more expensive, it's worth considering if you are planning on venturing forth into a remote location for a longer period of time.

Leave no trace: The great outdoors is something to be enjoyed by everyone, but to keep the natural world healthy and thriving, we have a responsibility to minimise our impact on it as much as we can. This means leaving as few traces of your presence as possible: take all your litter home with you, extinguish and cover up your campfires, dismantle any shelters you have built, and if you are foraging or using wood for fire or shelter, make sure you only take what you need and don't take too much from one area.

Tell me, what is it you plan to do with your one wild and precious life?

MARY OLIVER

CAMpING

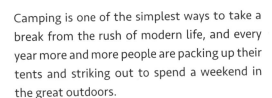

Camping is one of the simplest ways to take a break from the rush of modern life, and every year more and more people are packing up their tents and striking out to spend a weekend in the great outdoors.

Instead of the harsh alert of your alarm clock, the soft light of the rising sun is your wake-up call. As you take your first steps of the day and rub bleariness from your eyes, you're greeted with birdsong, the rustle of leaves in the trees and lungfuls of fresh air. A change of location can be just what you need to refresh and recharge.

Whether you're embarking on a wild camping trip or pitching your tent in a campsite, here is a list of the essentials that no camper should be without:

> **A tent.** Wild camping will require the most lightweight tent you can find, as you will be walking with it, along with all your other belongings, but if you're driving to a campsite you can afford to bring something bigger.

> **A sleeping bag appropriate for the season.** Many sleeping bags cover two or more seasons, so will be fine for most trips, but always check to see if the bag will suit the environment and temperatures you're likely to experience.

> **A sleeping mat.** Having a layer between you and the ground will conserve heat and make your night a lot more comfortable.

> **Warm layers.** Always bring a warm jumper with you, but remember to pack plenty of thinner layers as well. Worn together, these will trap a lot of extra heat, and it's easier to regulate your temperature.

> **Compostable bags/bin bags.** These are always useful, whether it's to keep your boots dry overnight, or to keep your litter in.

> **A torch.** Useful for locating things at night and finding your way to the toilet in the dark.

> **String/cord.** You never know when string or cord might come in handy, whether it's to use as a makeshift washing line or to tie something together.

> **Cooking supplies.** Decide what kind of food you will be cooking before you go and prepare as much as you can in advance. The minimum you are likely to need is: some form of camping stove and fuel, matches (kept waterproof), a pot to cook your food in, utensils for cooking and eating, and a tin opener.

> **Toilet roll.** If you're on a campsite you can't guarantee that the toilet block will be well stocked and it's always good to be prepared.

The man who goes afoot, prepared to camp anywhere and in any weather, is the most independent fellow on Earth.

HORACE KEPHART

LIGHTING A FIRE

It's human instinct to feel drawn to flames as a source of warmth and safety. Being able to gather round a fire helped us to develop as a social species, so it's no wonder that experiencing a campfire still feels so enjoyable and natural, even today.

A fire engages all your senses – the hypnotic glow of the fierce orange flames, the wall of heat, the smell of smoke and the snap and crackle of wood as it burns – and it draws your focus. This mesmerising effect, especially if it's experienced in a group, reduces anxiety and makes us feel peaceful. In recent years, the calming effect of sitting round a campfire has also been scientifically proven to lower blood pressure. Building a campfire is therefore arguably an essential part of any camping trip and will create memories that last. It's also easy to do once you know how.

How to light a fire

1. Find an area with plenty of space which is several metres away from trees, bushes and overhanging branches. Clear the ground as much as you can before placing any fuel down – there should be no flammable material, such as small leaves or twigs, in the vicinity. Make sure you have a source of water to hand to put your fire out as well.

2. Use rocks or large stones to make a ring around where you will have your fire. Preferably use hard rocks (rather than soft or layered rocks) for this, and check that they are dry. If the ground is damp, make a raft-like structure with dry twigs in the middle of the ring to raise the fire off the damp ground.

3. You will then need to gather tinder, kindling and fuel. Tinder is fast-burning and easy to ignite, like dry grass or newspaper (see p.31 on how to make your own tinder). Kindling should also be easy to light but longer lasting than grass, such as large twigs or cardboard. For fuel, look for (or bring with you) a variety of sticks and logs, some with a small thumb-sized diameter and some the thickness of your arm.

4. First, place the tinder in the middle of the ring of stones, then arrange the kindling on top of it in a teepee shape, leaving a small gap so you can ignite it. To keep your fire a manageable size, this structure shouldn't be wider than your handspan.

5. Light a match or lighter, or use a fire starter to ignite the tinder. You may need to blow lightly on the tinder to help the flame catch. Once your kindling is burning well, add the sticks and logs gradually to the outside of the fire over an extended period of time, starting with the smallest pieces of wood and working up to the largest logs.

6. To extinguish the fire, let it burn down. Then pour copious amounts of water over it until any remaining flames are out. With a stick or other implement, scrape any fuel that's partially burned to make sure there are no more hot embers. Then mix the ashes and embers together and ensure everything is wet so it can't reignite. Once everything is completely cool to the touch, break up the ground beneath your campfire with a stick, distribute the cold, wet ashes discreetly and cover the site with leaves or other natural debris. The area should look just as you found it before you leave.

HOW TO COOK OVER A CAMPFIRE

You will need a tree saw or folding saw for this, and a cooking pot with a bucket-like handle.

> Use the saw to cut two tree limbs, about 5 centimetres in diameter and a metre long, each with a 'Y' shape at the end. Then cut a green limb approximately the same length and thickness but with no 'Y' shape (green wood will be heavier than dead wood, its bark will not peel away and it may have moss or other fungi growing on it). It is important that this limb is green so it's less flammable.

> Before lighting your fire, take the two Y-shaped sticks and drive them into the ground (with a mallet, if you've brought one), one either side of your fire ring. Ensure the distance between them isn't greater than the length of your green limb. Next, hook the cooking pot's handle over your green limb and balance it in the grooves of the Y-shaped sticks. You may need to adjust the height of the two planted limbs to ensure your pot is close enough to the heat source.

> Once you're sure your structure is stable, remove the green limb with the cooking pot hanging on it and proceed to light your fire.

I JUST NEED
TO GO
Camping

CAMPING-STOVE COOKING

You don't have to light a campfire to be able to cook up a storm in the wild; a camping stove will do the job just as well. Light and portable, these handy devices will mean that you're able to have a hot meal after a day's adventuring wherever you are – a simple pleasure that really is second to none.

Using a camping stove usually means carrying some form of gas with you, so it's important to be sure that you're handling it correctly and safely. Canisters should only ever be in the camping stove when you're using it. Otherwise, your fuel should be kept in a dry place, away from the stove and in an upright position.

Camping stoves work best when they're on a flat surface, so spend time finding the perfect spot, or you could build a level platform with rocks and sticks (as long as it's sturdy). Try to pick a spot that has reasonable shelter from the wind, otherwise you'll have a tricky time getting the gas to light.

When choosing your cooking pot, go for something that's as close to the size of your burner ring as possible, or a little bigger, as this will use your energy the most efficiently. If possible, make sure your pot has a lid so that you can trap as much heat as possible.

To save cooking time, soak foods such as pasta and rice for 5–10 minutes in cold water before you add them to the boiling pan, as this will reduce the time needed over the flame.

When you've finished cooking, give the stove enough time to cool down before you try to remove the gas cartridge or canister.

BUILDING YOUR OWN CAMPING STOVE

This is a project to get stuck into during the cold winter nights when you are at home planning your adventures. You will need two empty aluminium food cans. One should be able to fit inside the other. Make sure they are clean and dry, with their labels and one lid removed (with a can opener) on each. Be careful of any sharp edges.

1. Take the larger can and invert it so that the base is facing up. Place the smaller can on top and draw a ring around it on to the base of the large can. Remove this middle section on the large can with sheet metal shears and file the edges smooth.

2. Turn the larger can the right way up and then drill a line of holes with a small drill bit around the bottom perimeter. Then drill another ring of holes just above that, lining up with the spaces in the first row. Enlarge all the holes with a bigger drill bit.

3. Then take the small can and use a small drill bit to add holes all over the base. They should be evenly spaced.

4. Then do the same as with the large can and drill two rings of holes around the bottom of the can's outside. Finally, drill a ring of smaller holes round the top edge of the small can.

Fill the small can with fuel – twigs, small pieces of cardboard, pine cones – and place the can inside the larger can.

Make sure the can is resting on soil, concrete or a heatproof surface and that you are outside. Then light the fuel with a match and you're ready to cook. If your fuel burns down mid-way through cooking, simply top it up.

COSY CAMPFIRE BEAN CHILLI Serves 2-3

INGREDIENTS

1 onion, diced
1 tbsp olive oil
1 can baked beans
1 can kidney beans in
   chilli sauce
1 can chopped tomatoes
1 tsp garlic powder
1 tsp chilli powder
   (or more to taste)
1 tsp paprika
Salt and pepper, to taste
Cheese, chopped spring
   onions and crusty bread
   to serve, optional

METHOD

Heat the oil in a pan (try to achieve a low heat), then add the onions and cook until translucent.

Add the baked beans, kidney beans and chopped tomatoes. Stir to combine. Add the garlic powder, chilli powder, paprika, stir thoroughly, then leave to simmer for 20 minutes.

Season to taste with salt and pepper, and serve topped with cheese and spring onions, with a hunk of crusty bread on the side.

Top tip: if you're planning on cooking meals while you're camping, prepare ahead of time and minimise fuss by decanting your required seasonings into one container for each meal.

CAMPFIRE S'MORES

>>> ──►

INGREDIENTS

Marshmallows
Rich tea biscuits
Toffee sauce
Chocolate

METHOD

Place your marshmallow on a long stick (see p.31) and roast over the campfire until it's just beginning to go gooey and golden brown.

Place the marshmallow on top of a rich tea biscuit. Drizzle with toffee sauce, add a couple of pieces of chocolate and top with another digestive to create a gooey, chocolatey delight.

CAMPFIRE KEBABS Makes 4

INGREDIENTS

1 yellow pepper, cut into
  bite-sized chunks
1 red pepper, cut into
  bite-sized chunks
8 small mushrooms
1 aubergine, cut into
  bite-sized chunks
1 courgette, sliced
8 cherry/plum tomatoes
1 tbsp olive oil
Lemon juice (optional)
Salt and pepper
4 extra-long skewers
  (whittled or shop bought)

METHOD

If you are whittling your skewers, make them exactly as you would for a marshmallow stick (see p.31) but with more of the bark stripped off above the tip.

Wash and prepare the vegetables. You could do this ahead of time to minimise fuss while you camp.

Thread the vegetables on to the kebab skewers, alternating so you get at least two pieces of each ingredient per skewer.

Drizzle with olive oil and lemon juice (if using) and season.

Roast over the campfire for 5 minutes, or until the vegetables are softening.

BUiLDiNG A SHELTER

>>> ———————————————————▶

Building a shelter is easy when you know what to look for, and the skill isn't just useful for keeping you dry in a storm. They're great fun to build, and can make a cosy nook from which to watch the birds, a windbreak for your camping stove, or a sheltered space to sit and enjoy bathing in the calm of a forest.

The key piece of equipment is a tarpaulin or groundsheet, as this will be what forms your shelter. Other useful materials are lengths of cord/rope and tent pegs.

LET'S
GO
CAMPING

Method one

You will need a tarpaulin and tent pegs. Find two trees growing a few metres apart. Tie your cord/rope between the two of them, like a washing line. Then simply drape your tarpaulin over the rope and secure the outer corners to the ground with pegs or heavy rocks, and you've made yourself a shelter. As long as you angle the side of the shelter against the wind, this method would be particularly good for wet-weather protection.

Method two

For this you'll need to find four trees roughly in a square position. You'll also need your tarpaulin, tent pegs and cord/rope (including two shorter lengths). Repeat the steps in method one, tying a cord/rope between two trees like a washing line and draping the tarpaulin over it. Secure one side of the tarpaulin on the ground where it falls with your pegs. Then lift the other side so it's 90 degrees from the ground and secure each corner to the other two trees with your shorter lengths of cord/rope. This allows you a good view out of the shelter, and acts as an effective windbreak if you are trying to cook on a camping stove.

Method three

For this shelter you will need three long, straight branches (two of them approximately 2 metres and one a little shorter), tent pegs and a length of cord/rope. Take your two longer branches and drive them into the ground at an angle to form a triangle shape. They should cross over slightly at the top. Then take the shorter branch. Rest one end in the cradle formed by the two standing branches, and drive the other end into the ground. Drape the tarpaulin over the top of the structure. Then secure the top (where the branches cross over) with cord/rope and the bottom with tent pegs.

FINDING WATER

>>> ————————————————————➤

We all know that staying hydrated is key to our health, but being able to find water is one of the most important survival skills there is: although humans can survive three weeks without food, we can only last three days without water. Knowing where to find that vital H_2O and how to make it safe to drink will boost your confidence as an outdoor explorer and furnish you with essential skills to help you thrive in the wild.

How to find water

Water will always run downwards, so starting your search by finding lower ground is a smart move. You could also look out for the surrounding wildlife: if there are tracks around you, or lots of signs of life, it's likely that there is a water source somewhere nearby.

How to collect water

If you can't find water, there are numerous ways to collect it. If it's raining, attach a tarpaulin between several trees and angle it so that the water it collects runs down into a bucket. If it's early morning, tie T-shirts to your legs and run through dewy grass. The T-shirts will collect the moisture which you can squeeze out into a receptacle.

How to purify water

Water collected in the wild runs the risk of being contaminated with mud, bacteria or chemicals, so unless you have collected it from a high-altitude, fast-running stream and you're confident that it's safe to drink, you should always purify it.

You can use a shop-bought water filter for this, or purification tablets. Alternatively, you can make your own simple filter. All you need is a sock and a few materials from the environment around you. Take the sock and layer it with sand, small pebbles and finally straw. Then pour your water through this makeshift filter, remembering to catch it at the bottom. By doing this, the turbidity – the mud, soil, grit, etc. – will be removed. Then boil the water on a rolling boil in a pot with a lid for at least 4 minutes to kill any remaining bacteria.

WHITTLING AND CARVING

>>>————————————————————————————————▶

A large part of bushcraft is the ability to use the environment around you to help you survive, like being able to create what you need by whittling (carving and shaving layers off) branches and sticks. With your own two hands, you can make all manner of things come into being: cups, spoons, fire starters and even tent pegs.

You will need a knife for all of the following. There is a variety to choose from, including penknives and folding knives, but a fixed-blade knife (with a protective sheath for when it's not in use) is possibly the safest to use, as there's no risk of the blade folding back on itself. You can find whittling-specific knives at outdoor stores and online.

Shavings

Making shavings is a good way to practise your whittling skills to start off with, and the shavings make great kindling for a campfire (see p.14). Find a dry stick (already on the ground) and run your knife blade away from yourself down the edge of the stick, slowly and at a slight angle, shaving off small sections.

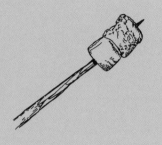

Marshmallow stick

Similar to the above, find a dry, moss-free stick from the surrounding area that's roughly the width of a pencil and approximately 50 centimetres long. Use your knife to take shavings off the tip of the stick, working your way round until you have a sharp point. Then shave off the outer bark to about 15 centimetres above the pointy end. Make sure there are no splinters, and your stick is ready for a session of marshmallow toasting.

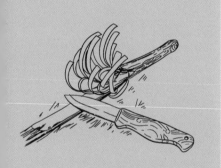

Feather stick

Once you've mastered the art of making shavings, try a feather stick. Do just as you would do with normal shavings, but stop your knife just before the shaving becomes detached, so you create a curl or 'feather'. Continue doing this on one side of the stick until you have something that resembles a feather duster. These make great tinder if dry grass is in short supply.

Tent peg

If you want to make something a little bigger, try carving a tent peg. For this you will need a camping or folding saw in addition to your knife. Begin by searching for thick sticks approximately 20 centimetres long and 3 centimetres in diameter. Use your knife to sharpen one end into a point. Then measure approximately 5 centimetres down from the unsharpened end and use your saw to cut roughly a quarter of the way through the stick. Switch to your knife and make another cut at a 45-degree angle to the saw mark. This is the notch that the tent rope will sit in. Finally, use the knife to round off the top of the peg, as this will stop the peg splitting when you hammer it into the ground.

FORAGING

>>>———————————————————————▶

Historically, humans evolved to be hunter-gatherers and relied on foraging to provide enough food to survive. It's a skill that many of us have no need for today, but foraging is a great way to learn about the natural world and to get back in touch with it. Plus, it's highly rewarding – like a real-life treasure hunt where the prize is a delicious dish that you'll have found and cooked for yourself from scratch. From ideas including easy-to-find leaves and berries, to foods that require more of a search, several recipes for foraged ingredients appear in the following pages. Here are the golden rules which apply to any and every foraging trip:

> If you're not absolutely confident that what you've found is edible, then under no circumstances should you eat it. If you would like guidance, take a field guide with you when you forage.

> Some wild herbs and plants could react with medication, so if you are taking anything check with your doctor first before foraging.

> Always gain permission from the landowner before foraging.

> If you're trying something for the first time, ensure that you're in a safe environment and have another person with you in case you experience an allergic reaction.

> When foraging, don't take too much from one area, as this will harm the plant populations. Forage from as wide an area as possible, and don't take any more than you need.

> Be vigilant for areas that could have been sprayed with pesticides. Plants that grow at roadsides, for example, are often sprayed. As always, if you're not sure, err on the side of caution and don't forage in that area.

LIFE IS BETTER BY THE CAMPFIRE

FORESTS & WOODLANDS

Step into a forest, and you step into a different world. A forest is quiet, majestic and mysterious, but also bursting with colour and life. There is something to discover wherever you look, whether it's in the green canopy above or on the floor underfoot. Among the trees you can walk, relax, climb or explore – the forest is a realm of possibility.

FOREST BATHING

A forest is a place of stillness and calm, somewhere the noise and bustle of daily life can't quite reach. It's a peaceful, natural space where you can unwind, refresh and restore yourself.

This idea – that the forest has the power to heal – is at the heart of the Japanese practice of forest bathing, *shinrin-yoku*. The concept is simple: walk through the forest, take your time and absorb the atmosphere around you. The clean, green air. Sunlight. Birdsong. The wind in the trees. The ground under your feet. As you wander, focus only on this and allow your mind to switch off and relax.

There are many health benefits of forest bathing. It can boost your immune system; reduce blood pressure; increase your energy levels; improve your mood, your sleep and your ability to focus; and even accelerate your body's ability to heal. Studies have also shown that, when measured, rates of hostility and aggression diminish among those who have been in a forest environment. Being at one with nature, surrounded by a naturally beautiful ambience, promotes positivity and happiness.

Come to the woods,
for here is rest.
There is no repose like
that of the green deep woods.

JOHN. MUIR

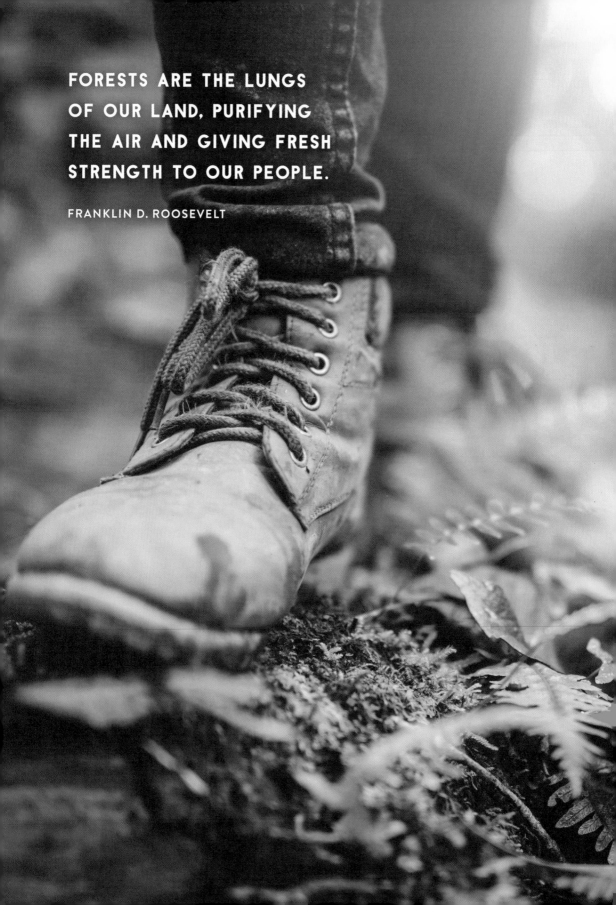

FORESTS ARE THE LUNGS
OF OUR LAND, PURIFYING
THE AIR AND GIVING FRESH
STRENGTH TO OUR PEOPLE.

FRANKLIN D. ROOSEVELT

WOODLAND WALKS

»——————————————————▶

Walking is a restorative joy that people have celebrated for hundreds of years. In an age of speed, convenience and technology, there's nothing quite like the simple pleasure of striding through green, woody spaces to make you feel refreshed.

SPEND TIME WITH TREES

>>>———————————————▶

Get in touch with nature – literally! As you walk through forest and woodland, reach out to feel the world around you: the texture of leaves, the soft petal of a flower, or perhaps the water of a stream. Particularly soothing are the trees. Even just being in their presence can have a calming effect, but it's been proven that spending a few minutes hugging a tree can bring you real health benefits too, such as reducing stress, and improving your mental well-being by giving you a sense of positivity, confidence and calm.

Wrap your arms around the trunk of a tree and link your fingers if you can. Rest your cheek against the bark, close your eyes and feel your heartbeat slow. Feel the stillness and steadiness of the tree, imagine both its roots anchored into the ground and the branches that reach upwards. Soon this feeling of being grounded will transfer to you.

It is not so much for its beauty that the forest makes a claim upon men's hearts, as for that subtle something, that quality of air that emanates from old trees, that so wonderfully changes and renews a weary spirit.

ROBERT LOUIS STEVENSON

Trees are poems that the Earth writes upon the sky.

KAHLIL GIBRAN

THE WORLD IS YOURS

SPIRIT OF
FREEDOM

TREE CLIMBING

If you're looking for the thrill of adventure, reach for new heights and try tree climbing.

Find a tree with sturdy, low branches, and clamber over and around them, noticing the new perspectives you get even from just a few feet of difference in height. Or, if you want more of a challenge, you could try recreational tree climbing. Companies that offer this will be able to provide you with safety gear and ropes which allow you to scale the tallest trees – you will feel your spirit soar as you survey the forest from high above.

Climbing a tree is the perfect way to embrace what the forest has to offer, and this great year-round activity has the added benefit of improving your muscle strength and giving you a sense of accomplishment too.

Note: Do not climb trees on your own. Always ensure that the tree is safe to climb and can hold your weight. Never climb higher than you can safely get down from.

If you would know strength and patience,
welcome the company of trees.

HAL BORLAND

ORiENTEERiNG

>>>————————————————▶

For those who thrive on a bit of healthy competition, orienteering is the perfect activity to get involved in. This adventure sport involves getting from point A to B as quickly as possible, armed with only a map, a compass and your wits. You don't need any special equipment to take part; as long as you have a pair of sturdy shoes and suitable outdoor clothing, you're ready to go.

As well as being an exciting way to explore the landscape around you, orienteering hones your navigation skills – something that often gets neglected in the age of map-reading apps. It's also commonly a team sport, so taking part in events gives you the chance to meet and connect with new people.

If the idea – but not the competitive element – appeals, there are plenty of orienteering clubs which hold weekly sessions to allow you to practise the skill without the pressure of going against the clock.

NIGHT WALKING

>>>————————————————————————————————————>

A forest by the light of the moon is a whole different world to the forest in the day. It may feel ominous at first, but under the cover of darkness there's just as much activity to discover, and the forest itself is as enchanting and mysterious as ever.

Stay among the trees, close to the edge of the forest, and as the sun goes down watch the world turn from green to golden to dusky. Look closely for the nocturnal animals that make an appearance at twilight, such as badgers and hedgehogs. Listen for the rustles of mice and the bark of foxes. In the canopy above you may even catch a glimpse of bats or owls as they sweep across the sky. If you stay in the woods until night has completely fallen, notice how your night vision improves and your hearing sharpens, and absorb the busy atmosphere of the night-time forest.

The clearest way into
the Universe is through
a forest wilderness.

JOHN MUIR

TREETOP WALKS

Seek out a treetop walkway to enjoy a bird's-eye view of the forest. This unique perspective will allow you to enjoy breathtaking views from the very tops of the trees, and it's guaranteed to be an experience of the forest that you'll never forget.

sts are bursting with life, so if you want to catch a glimpse of an animal in the wild they're a
place to start. Finding and following animal tracks requires patience, but once you learn to
tify the clues it can be very rewarding. You'll be amazed at how much you can discover about
n the wild from just one animal track.

P TIPS FOR TRACKING

Look up the animals that are likely to inhabit the forests near you. What do their prints look like? What are the features of their habitats? What kind of food do they eat?

f you're tracking a particular animal, establish whether it is predator or prey. Its status in the food chain will have an effect on its activity and help you to narrow down where it might be.

The best time for tracking is early in the morning, or the late afternoon or early evening. Animals tend to be more active around these times of day, so you're more likely to see fresh tracks.

Some of the best clues are animal prints, which can be found in mud or puddles, or n scuffed dirt and leaves. When you find them, check the prints for the number of toes, the shape of the foot, or whether it has claws to identify what it is. Examine the print pattern to see how the animal was moving, as this also provides clues about the species. Bounding (four prints, where all the feet have landed in one clump) could mean ferrets; hopping (four prints, where

of the front feet) could mean rabbits; walking with staggered tracks (more similar to the pattern of human prints) could mean hoofed animals, such as deer.

> 'Animal tracks' are not just footprints – a track is made up of any evidence that an animal has left behind. This means that burrows and holes, scat, and any evidence of grazing, foraging or kill sites can also be helpful clues as to what you're following and where it might be.

> Check whether the trail you're following is old or new. New footprints and new scat will often be smoother around the edges, while older ones will be dry and cracked. If you're looking for displaced leaves and undergrowth, these will often appear darker than the surrounding area if they've been disturbed recently.

> Some animals will be easier to track than others – for instance, it's easier to find evidence of larger animals with heavy hoof-prints than it is to find soft-footed ones. As long as you're patient and keep looking, you're sure to spot an animal in

Rabbit tracks:

Deer tracks:

Badger tracks:

BiRDWATCHiNG

Birdwatching is truly one of life's simple pleasures. Find a spot to pause along a forest path, listen out and look around you – both up in the treetops and in the undergrowth. It might take a few minutes, but before long you're sure to spot all kinds of forest-dwelling birds going about their day-to-day lives.

Wild & Free

TOP TIPS FOR BIRDWATCHING

> Before you set out, look up the kinds of birds that inhabit the forests in your area, or invest in a field guide to help you identify the birds you see. Why not keep a record of your sightings and see how many you spot?

> Get in touch with your local birdwatching group. They will have the best information about the birdwatching hotspots and will often have tips about recent sightings. Although quiet, birdwatching can also be a social activity, and many birdwatchers will be more than happy to share their knowledge with you.

> Wear darker colours that will blend into the environment around you. This will give you camouflage, so the birds are more likely to be relaxed around you.

> Birdwatching can be especially rewarding if you have a pair of binoculars to see the birds more closely, but you don't have to have them; you can see many birds well with the naked eye.

> Bring your camera. Birds are beautiful creatures with so much character – snapping what you see will make a perfect keepsake.

> Always remember to be respectful to the birds and don't disturb them or their habitats. Stay on forest paths to avoid straying into their territory, don't get too close to them, and keep any noise to a minimum.

> If you see a bird in a nest, make especially sure to keep your distance as they are particularly sensitive. They could be scared away or become aggressive, both of which could have detrimental effects on the eggs or chicks in the nest.

Keep a green tree in your heart and perhaps
a singing bird will come.

CHINESE PROVERB

Forest treasures: wild garlic

Wild garlic grows in forests and woody areas in most parts of the northern hemisphere from around March to June. Due to its distinctive garlic scent you can usually smell it before you see it! Spear-shaped leaves give way to small clusters of white, star-shaped flowers, and they grow in great numbers, often carpeting the forest floor. Although picking wild flowers is generally frowned upon, due to this natural abundance, the removal of a few leaves and flowers from a wide area will not have a detrimental impact.

Both the leaves and flowers of wild garlic are edible. The leaves can be eaten raw or used in sauces and soups; the flowers, which bloom later in the season, make great additions to salads. There are also many health benefits associated with this plant: as well as containing vitamins A and C, calcium and iron, and having antibacterial properties, wild garlic is said to lower cholesterol and reduce blood pressure.

To harvest, pick the leaves and flowers of wild garlic plants using scissors or secateurs. Put cuttings into a plastic bag, taking care to be gentle as the leaves can bruise easily. Refrigerate them once you return home and keep them for up to a week.

Note: When foraging, beware: wild garlic looks very similar to lily of the valley, which is poisonous. Before harvesting what you think is garlic, always take one leaf of the plant and crush it between your fingers. If it smells like garlic, it's safe to use.

WiLD GARLiC PESTO Serves 4

INGREDIENTS

80 g wild garlic leaves
   (or more to taste)
30 g Parmesan, grated
30 g pine nuts
3 tbsp olive oil
Lemon juice, to taste
Salt and pepper
400 g fresh pasta or
   tomatoes, sliced, to serve

METHOD

Wash the garlic leaves thoroughly and pat dry.

Put the garlic, Parmesan, pine nuts and oil in a blender and blitz until smooth. Alternatively, crush by hand with a pestle and mortar.

Then add lemon juice, salt and pepper to taste. Add more oil if you prefer pesto with a thinner consistency.

Mix the pesto into fresh pasta and serve, or drizzle over sliced tomatoes for a zingy salad.

Forest treasures: elderflowers

Elderflowers come from the elder tree, and bloom in creamy-white sprays around June. They are most recognisable by their sweet, summery fragrance, which is especially noticeable on warm days.

The flowers and berries are the only edible parts of this plant, and they should always be cooked before consumption. They are perhaps most commonly used to make cordial, which is an excellent flavouring for drinks, jellies, ice cream, sauces, cakes and crumbles. Elderflower has also been used in traditional medicines for many years, and it is believed to have anti-inflammatory properties, so drinks containing the flower can also be a soothing balm for colds, flu or other respiratory ailments.

Be sure to smell the flowers before you pick them – as long as they smell sweet and fresh they will be fine to use. To harvest, cut the flower heads with scissors, or snap the heads off with your fingers, and put them in an open basket or hessian weeding bag. Never cover or tie up bags of harvested elderflowers, as this will cause them to sweat and become unusable.

Note: Be careful not to mistake cowbane for elderflowers, as this plant is poisonous. Cowbane grows from the ground, and the flowers at the end of the stem form multiple round sprays rather than one flat, umbrella-shaped spray.

ELDERFLOWER CORDIAL Makes approx. 1 litre

INGREDIENTS

20 elderflower heads
650 g caster sugar
1 litre water
Zest and juice of
　2 unwaxed lemons
Zest and juice of
　1 unwaxed lime

METHOD

Give the flower heads a good shake to rid them of any insects, then rinse them before using.

Simmer the water in a large pan then add the sugar until dissolved.

Remove pan from the heat, then add the zest and juice of the lemons and lime, and stir.

Add the elderflower heads to the pan, making sure that the flowers are submerged and the stalks are standing up out of the water. Then slice the remaining lemon rind and add it to the pan as well. Cover and leave to infuse overnight.

Strain the liquid through muslin or a good-quality tea towel, and store the cordial in bottles or jars for up to three weeks in the fridge.

Serve diluted with water or added to drinks such as Prosecco, white wine or gin.

Forest treasures: sweet chestnuts

The best time for foraging for sweet chestnuts is late autumn, which makes this delicious delicacy from the forest a perfect treat to enjoy when the nights are drawing in.

Sweet chestnuts can be cooked in a variety of ways and eaten either on their own (roasted) or in pies, soups and salads. They are high in dietary fibre, which helps to regulate cholesterol levels, and, unlike other nuts, they are low in protein and fat. Their richness in vitamin C also means that they are an antioxidant and contribute to a healthy immune system.

Sweet chestnuts are easy to distinguish from horse chestnuts (also known as conkers) because their shells are yellow and spiky – often described as looking like small hedgehogs – rather than green and thorny-looking.

To harvest, search the ground beneath sweet chestnut trees for cases that have fallen. You might want to bring gloves with you when you're foraging as the shells are very prickly. In their shells, chestnuts keep for a week at room temperature, but if you want to keep them any longer, refrigerate them in a paper bag for up to three weeks.

HOW TO ROAST CHESTNUTS

Preheat the oven to 200°C/390°F/gas mark 6.

Remove the nuts from the spiky shells and prepare them for cooking. Nuts can give a little if you squeeze them, but discard any that are soft. Also discard any nuts that have holes in them.

Place a nut flat-side down on a chopping board. With a serrated knife, carefully make a shallow incision all the way across the rounded surface. Do this on all the nuts. The slit should be deep enough to have cut through the skin – its purpose is to let the steam out when the nuts are in the oven, which stops them exploding.

Put the chestnuts cut-side up on a baking tray and roast them for 15–20 minutes, or until the skin begins to come away from the nut.

Peel the chestnuts as soon as you can once they're out of the oven, as they're easiest to peel when still warm. Use oven gloves or a cloth to protect your hands from the heat.

Serve the chestnuts as they are, or use them in salads, soups or pies. The cooked, peeled chestnuts can be kept in the fridge in an airtight container for up to four days, or frozen for up to three months.

LIFE IS A JOURNEY NOT A DESTINATION

MOUNTAINS & HILLSIDES

Mountain summits that stretch up into the clouds and shape our skyline remind us that nature is a beautiful and powerful place. High up on the rocky slopes, the world seems to open up before you – the clouds are at your feet and you can almost touch the sky. The side of a mountain is a place for both high energy and adventure, and for moments of tranquillity and awe.

CLOUD WATCHING

>>>———————————▶

They often go unnoticed, but if you take time to look up, you'll catch one of nature's most impressive and beautiful displays: the clouds. A sunny sky is often what we hope for when we're planning a day in the open, but a cloudy sky is infinitely more interesting. Every cloud is as unique as a snowflake. They are constantly evolving, and the ways they change and catch the light can create moments of striking, majestic beauty.

Clouds make a great display wherever you are, but from a mountainside the extra height can afford spectacular views that you don't get from the ground.

A field guide to clouds

Cirrus: Thin, wispy, high-level clouds, which often appear on sunny days and at sunrise and sunset.

Altostratus: A thin, mid-level layer of grey cloud which is spread over a wide area. The sun is often faintly visible through it.

Altocumulus: These mid-level clouds appear as fluffy patches, which make the sky look as if it has a thin covering of wool.

Cumulonimbus: Thick and billowing, these are storm clouds. They usually have a flat base which is fairly close to ground level, but tower high up into the sky. They can be white or grey.

Cumulus: Fluffy, rounded, picture-perfect clouds – usually bright white and appearing on sunny days.

Stratocumulus: Low-level cloud that gives the sky a wide, patchy cover. Spots of blue sky are usually visible through the gaps.

Stratus: Long, flat, uniform, grey clouds that hang low in the sky, creating overcast days. They appear as fog or mist at ground level.

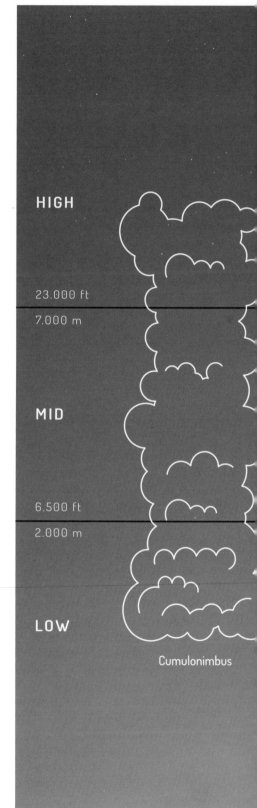

HIGH

23.000 ft
7.000 m

MID

6.500 ft
2.000 m

LOW

Cumulonimbus

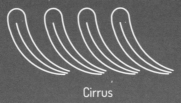

Cirrus

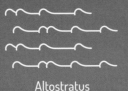

Altostratus

Cumulus

Altocumulus

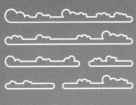

Stratus

Stratocumulus

PARAGLIDING AND HANG-GLIDING

Humankind has always longed to fly, and with a leap of faith, anybody can take to the skies with paragliding and hang-gliding. As you can fly in tandem with a professional, these incredible activities are not limited to those with experience, and you will be free to sit back and enjoy the breathtaking ride. As the ground falls away from beneath your feet, experience the sense of liberation and leaving your worries far, far below as you drift on the air currents over mountains, hills and valleys.

73

SNOW YOGA

>>>————————————————————————————————————►

Winter weather doesn't have to stop you from making the most of the great outdoors. Embrace the cold and take your yoga practice outside: fill your lungs with fresh, crystalline air, drink in the wonderful views, and find your bliss among snow-capped hills and trees.

Be mindful of the cold, as this will affect your body's ability to move. For this reason, the best poses for snow yoga are standing poses that focus on balance and core strength, such as tree pose, eagle pose and the warrior poses. As long as you wear plenty of flexible layers to keep your body temperature up, and you have a good warm-up and cool-down, you're sure to have a safe and invigorating practice.

Being out in the snow has a positive effect on your mood. A snowy landscape can also bring a sense of stillness and calm, and seeing the familiar in an unfamiliar way allows us to refresh our perspectives on our own lives. The transience of snow also brings us into the present moment and reminds us of the beauty that can be found in the natural world.

Mountains are the
beginning and the end of
all natural scenery.

JOHN RUSKIN

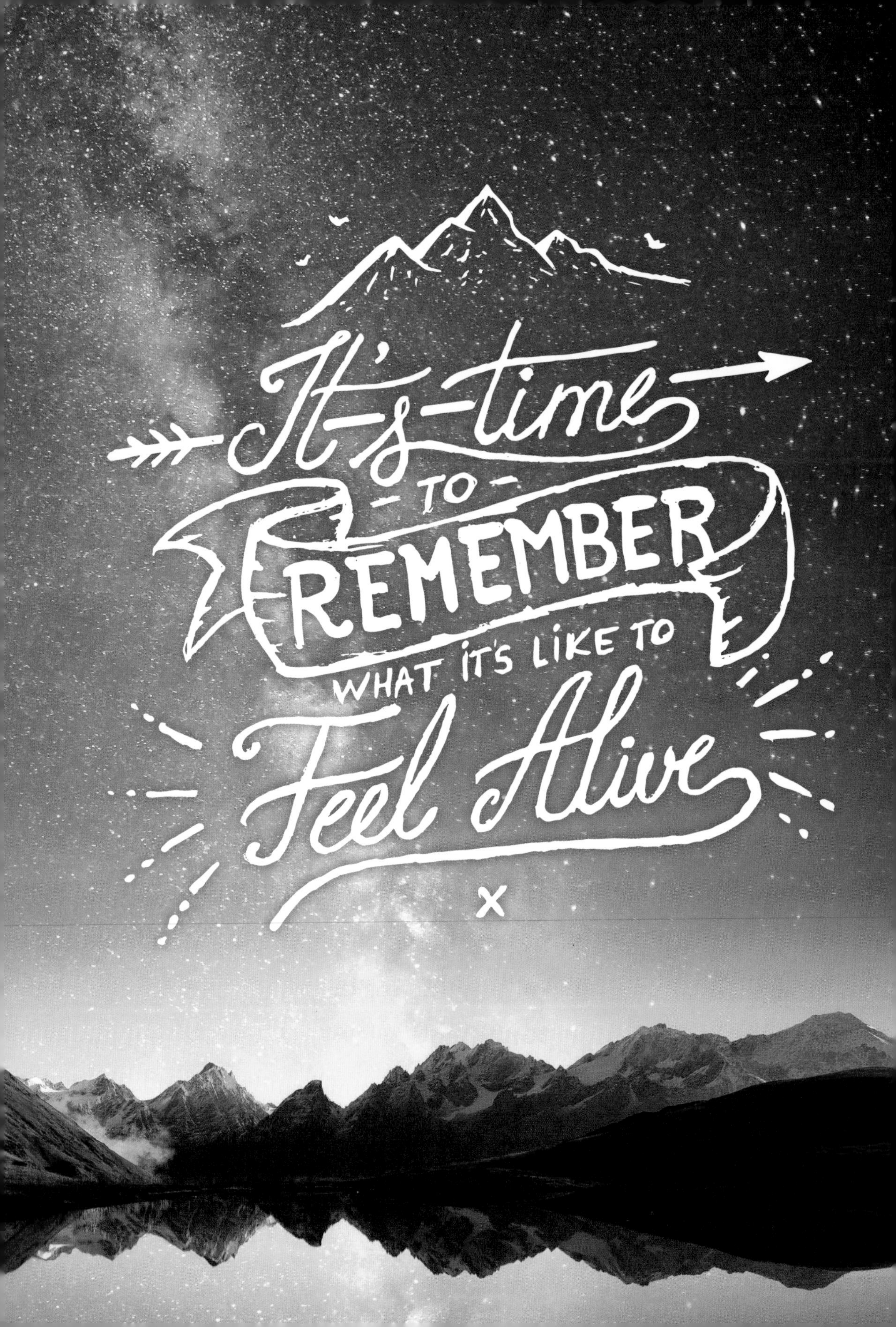
It's time
to
REMEMBER
what it's like to
Feel Alive
x

BivouACkiNG

>>> ───➤

Imagine being woken by the first rays of sunlight at the top of a mountain. You open your eyes and there's no roof over your head, not even a tent – just the clouds and the sky, the golden light of the morning sun all around, and nothing for miles but rolling landscape.

Bivouacking – or 'bivvying' – is camping without the tent. The key piece of equipment is a bivvy bag – a breathable bag that you can use like a cocoon around your sleeping bag to keep you dry. It's also simple: when you decide it's bedtime, put your sleeping mat and sleeping bag inside the bivvy bag, climb in and go to sleep.

The advantage of bivvying is that it can be done anywhere, as long as you have a space wide enough to lie down on. This means it's particularly useful if you're exploring mountains, where there is often not enough room to pitch a tent.

Bivvying gives you a huge amount of freedom: if you want to sleep at the summit of a mountain, you can. It does require specialist equipment and forethought, and it can be uncomfortable, but the spectacular views and the memories you will get in return are worth the effort – you can't get much closer to nature than this.

YOU WILL NEED:

> A waterproof, breathable bivvy bag

> A sleeping bag that suits the climate

> A sleeping mat

> A large waterproof bag (to keep spare kit dry during the night)

> Plenty of food and water

> Appropriate clothing for hiking

> A warm hat and gloves

> A waterproof, breathable jacket

Let YOUR MEMORY BE YOUR travel BAG

Life is either a daring adventure or nothing.

HELEN KELLER

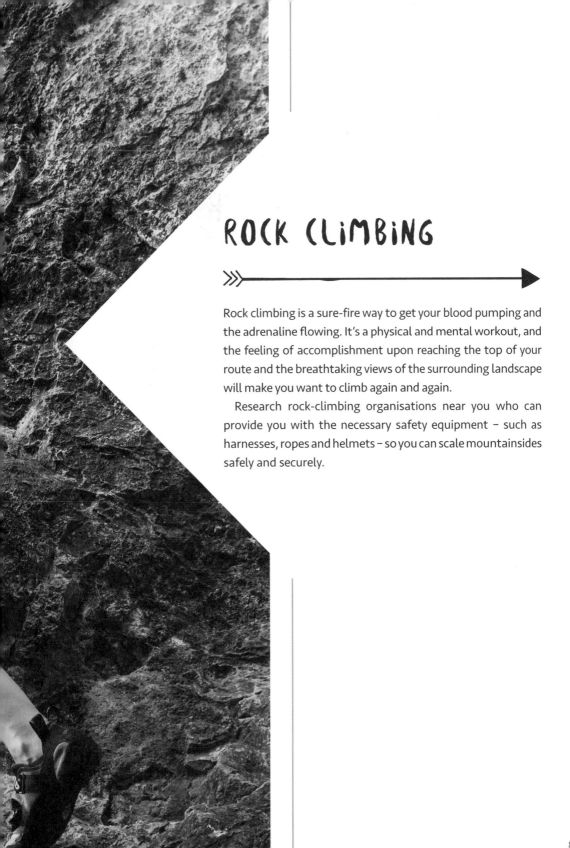

ROCK CLIMBING

Rock climbing is a sure-fire way to get your blood pumping and the adrenaline flowing. It's a physical and mental workout, and the feeling of accomplishment upon reaching the top of your route and the breathtaking views of the surrounding landscape will make you want to climb again and again.

Research rock-climbing organisations near you who can provide you with the necessary safety equipment – such as harnesses, ropes and helmets – so you can scale mountainsides safely and securely.

MOUNTAINEERING

If you want adventure, excitement, awe-inspiring views and an experience you'll never forget, climb a mountain.

Climbing a mountain is a challenge for both your body and your mind. The first steps can be particularly daunting; when you see the peak towering over you, it's hard to escape the thought of how far you have to go. But if you persevere, you will be rewarded. As well as improving your coordination and sense of balance, climbing a mountain can boost your confidence and focus, it can help to reduce stress, and it gives you an enormous sense of satisfaction and fulfilment.

TOP TIPS FOR MOUNTAINEERING

> **Join a trip:** Unless you're an experienced mountaineer, it's best to join an organised trip to ensure your own safety.

> **Preparation is key:** Familiarise yourself with your route before leaving and make sure you have the correct equipment.

> **Find your footwear:** Make sure you have appropriate footwear. Walking boots can often be used if climbing in the summer, otherwise invest in proper mountaineering boots which can cope with icy conditions.

> **Plan your emergency shelter:** The weather on mountains is unpredictable and dangerous if you are not prepared. Always carry some form of emergency shelter, such as a bothy bag, to protect you from the elements.

> **Assess your fitness:** Mountaineering requires physical exertion, and will more than likely include steep inclines and descents, scrambling and plenty of uneven ground, so before you set off ensure you're fit enough to take on the challenge, otherwise you could put yourself and others at risk.

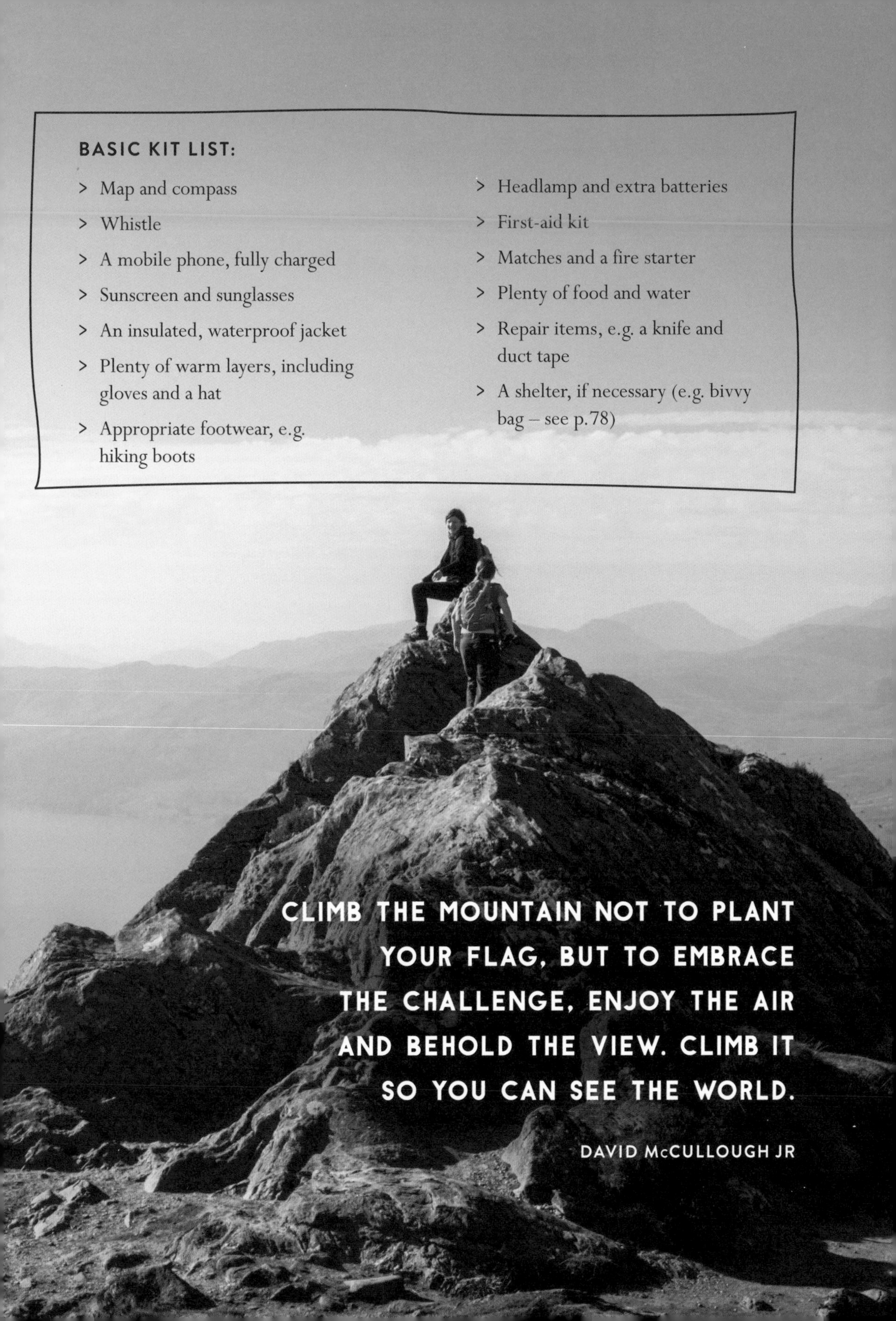

BASIC KIT LIST:

> Map and compass

> Whistle

> A mobile phone, fully charged

> Sunscreen and sunglasses

> An insulated, waterproof jacket

> Plenty of warm layers, including gloves and a hat

> Appropriate footwear, e.g. hiking boots

> Headlamp and extra batteries

> First-aid kit

> Matches and a fire starter

> Plenty of food and water

> Repair items, e.g. a knife and duct tape

> A shelter, if necessary (e.g. bivvy bag – see p.78)

CLIMB THE MOUNTAIN NOT TO PLANT
YOUR FLAG, BUT TO EMBRACE
THE CHALLENGE, ENJOY THE AIR
AND BEHOLD THE VIEW. CLIMB IT
SO YOU CAN SEE THE WORLD.

DAVID McCULLOUGH JR

ABSEILING

If you like to walk the paths less travelled, try abseiling. Abseiling is a technique that allows climbers and mountaineers to descend faces of rock that are too steep to climb. It can also be done for pleasure – for the sheer exhilaration of it.

If you are bold enough to take those first steps, you'll experience unparalleled views of the landscape and a wild, heart-thumping descent down the side of a mountain – and all while suspended by a single rope. It can be a challenge even for those with a head for heights, but when you conquer your fear you'll feel on top of the world.

Abseiling packs an adrenaline punch, but it's suitable for almost everyone. Some safety training is required for this activity so before you abseil unsupervised, find an adventure centre near you that can offer you equipment and guidance, and dare to push yourself beyond your comfort zone.

It is only in adventure
that some people succeed
in knowing themselves –
in finding themselves.

ANDRÉ GIDE

FELL RUNNING

Fell running is the wilder cousin of mountain and trail running, and if you enjoy finding your limits and then pushing beyond them, this sport could be for you. Although all of the above involve running over remote or rugged terrain, fell running is the most extreme.

Generally, the routes are unmarked, leaving you free to determine your own way from point A to B, so the sport is as much about navigation as it is about the act of running. What also makes it extreme is the terrain; as you're not confined to paths or tracks, you could contend with any combination of grass, paths, rocks, mud, scree, boggy ground, steep climbs and sharp descents on your route.

It's a tough sport, and not for the faint-hearted, but for those who rise to the challenge it's an exhilarating way to experience mountainous landscapes and incredibly rewarding.

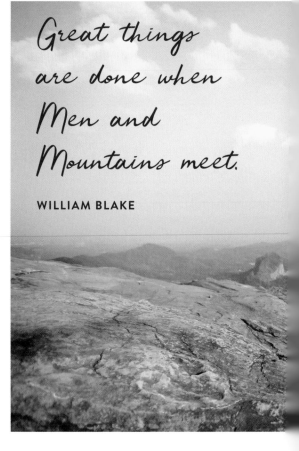

Great things are done when Men and Mountains meet.

WILLIAM BLAKE

TOP TIPS FOR FELL RUNNING

> Invest in proper fell-running shoes. These specialist shoes are needed to cope with the rough and varied terrain, to give you additional grip and to reduce the risk of injury.

> Always be prepared. In cold weather conditions, bring waterproof layers, a hat and gloves. And for your safety, always carry a map, compass and whistle.

> Always consider your route in advance — even if you decide to change and adapt it while you're running, you need to have an idea of where you're going.

> Consider joining a fell-running club. A club will allow you to run routes with other people, and they will have plenty of information about your local area. This is an especially good option for people starting out in the sport.

MOUNTAIN BIKING

Mountain biking is a hard and fast, quick-thinking adventure sport to get the adrenaline pumping and the blood flowing round your body. You can experience the most incredible landscapes while conquering the toughest terrain, and for those who dare to take on the hills, the sense of elation is immense.

The main trails for casual mountain bikers are cross-country and downhill routes. Cross-country is as it sounds – over all manners of terrain that the country offers, including water, grass and tracks. These routes are about strength and endurance. Downhill courses are fast dashes from the top of a hill to the bottom.

They require nerve and skill, and are not for the faint of heart.

Mountain biking can be tough, but it's a workout like no other. It gets your heart rate up, strengthens your arms, legs and torso, improves your lung performance, boosts your metabolism and even improves your reflexes. Many bikers also swear by the sport for improving their well-being and credit it with giving them a more positive outlook on the world.

It's a sport that can be done alone or in a group, but even if you're cycling solo it can be a great way to make new connections as you're sure to pass other bikers on the route, and everyone is connected by a love for the sport. If you're starting out, look up mountain bike trail centres where you'll be able to rent bikes and gear, and get expert advice on which kind of route to take.

It is in the compelling zest of high adventure and of victory, and in creative action, that man finds his supreme joys.

ANTOINE DE SAINT-EXUPÉRY

Mountain treasures: rowan berries

The rowan tree – or mountain ash – is a small tree that can often be found at high altitudes. It bears small white flowers in the spring and bright clusters of red-orange berries in the early autumn. Rowan trees are hardy and, if allowed the right conditions, can live for up to 200 years.

The berries are edible once cooked. They are often used to make jellies and jams as an accompaniment for other foods, or to flavour drinks. Rowan berries are packed with vitamin C, and they have also been used in traditional herbal remedies, particularly to help regulate digestion (as they are fibrous) and to ease respiratory problems by reducing inflammation.

To harvest, clip sprays of ripe berries from the tree and store in a breathable bag to bring them back with you. While foraging, bear in mind that berries from the rowan tree are particular favourites of birds, so while it's fine to take a few home with you, take care not to harvest too many so as not to deprive the surrounding wildlife of their food.

ROWAN BERRY JAM Makes 1 small jar

>>> ————————————————————————————————→

INGREDIENTS

150 g ripe rowan berries
2 firm eating apples
300 g white granulated
  sugar (approx.)
¼ tsp salt

METHOD

Wash the berries and remove the stalks then freeze them overnight. This will help to allay the sour taste of the berries.

Peel and dice the apples and put them in a large saucepan along with the frozen rowan berries. Just cover the fruit with cold water.

Bring the pan to the boil and then simmer until the fruit is soft – usually about 30–40 minutes.

Strain the fruit to separate the pulp from the seeds and skin of the rowan berries.

Measure the amount of strained fruit, then add this amount of sugar to a large saucepan. Then add the fruit and the salt.

Stir over a medium heat until the sugar has dissolved, then bring the pan to the boil for a couple of minutes. The sugar should begin to caramelise.

Test whether the jam is ready by putting a small spoonful on to a cold plate or surface. Wait a few moments for it to cool, then push it with a spoon. If it has set or forms wrinkles then the jam is ready.

Decant the rowan berry jam into a sterilised jar and serve with roast meats. Store it in the fridge for up to two months.

Mountain treasures: bilberries

Bilberries – also known as European blueberries or huckleberries – are little blue-black berries that grow on small, wiry shrubs on high ground. You'd be forgiven for confusing it with a blueberry, but the two fruits are different. Whereas blueberries are light green inside, bilberries have a deep blue-purple-coloured flesh, and are much juicier.

Bilberries have a sour taste, and although they can be eaten on their own, they're usually more enjoyable when they've been cooked – in jams, pies, sauces and cakes. In some circles they are also considered a superfood due to their health properties. Bilberries are naturally rich in anthocyanosides, which are powerful antioxidants and can also help to improve night vision. The nutrients of bilberries can improve circulation and help to regulate the body's blood sugar levels.

If you want to forage for bilberries, they can be found in late summer and early autumn. However, they don't grow in great quantities, so they can be hard to find. If you're lucky enough to spot some, you might find it takes time to pick the berries by hand, but their deliciously tart taste and unique health properties make them well worth it.

BiLBERRY MUFFiNS Makes 8–10

INGREDIENTS

100 g butter
150 g white caster sugar
2 eggs
Zest of 1 lemon
1 tsp vanilla essence
100 ml milk
280 g plain flour
2 tsp baking powder
Pinch of salt
100 g bilberries, washed

METHOD

Preheat the oven to 160°C/320°F/gas mark 3 and line a muffin tin with paper cases.

Put the butter and sugar in a large bowl and beat until the mixture is light and fluffy. Then add the egg, lemon zest and vanilla essence, and beat again until combined.

Add the milk to the mixture and beat until it is fully incorporated.

In a separate bowl, sieve the flour, baking powder and salt, and stir together. Then add it into the wet ingredients and fold it in with a metal spoon until combined. Then stir in the bilberries.

Divide the mixture between the muffin cases and bake for 25–35 minutes, or until the tops are golden and a skewer comes out clean.

Remove from the tin and allow the muffins to cool on a rack. Keep in an airtight container for up to a week.

BE UNCONVENTIONAL

SEAS

The ocean is a treasure trove of wonders waiting to be discovered and explored, full of deep-sea secrets and teeming with life. Whether we experience it from the top of a blustery cliff, from the shelter of a sandy cove, or from the rush of a surfboard, the ocean has the power to inspire, refresh and restore us.

SAND SCULPTURE

Think of your earliest childhood memories and it's likely that they will feature happy trips to the beach. There is a special joy in finding the perfect sand, packing a bucket full to the brim, turning it quickly over on to the beach and waiting with bated breath as the bucket lifts to reveal a smooth-sided sandcastle.

Recreate your childhood memories next time you go to the beach and take delight in the simple pleasure of making row upon row of beautiful sandcastles. Or, if you want to be more adventurous, why not try your hand at sand sculpture?

Sand sculpture is sandcastle-building taken to the next level. Instead of using a bucket, you create your own structure out of sand, and you can shape it any way you feel like. Build shapes, castles, animals – it's up to you. Down in the sand, you can forget neatness and you can let go of perfect. Instead, revel in getting your hands (and quite probably the rest of you) well and truly sandy! There's nothing like the pure happiness that comes from – literally – getting in touch with your creativity and the world around you.

TOP TIPS FOR SAND SCULPTING

> The best kind of sand to build with has fine grains that will compact tightly together. If the sand feels hard when you walk on it, it's likely to be good for sculpting.

> Choose your spot wisely – build above the tideline so that your sculpture won't be washed away! You'll be able to tell where the last tide came up to by looking for a line of seaweed, shells and beach debris.

> The key to building great sculptures is wet sand (imagine the texture of wet cement). Take buckets of seawater and sluice it over the sand that you're planning to use.

> Make sure your sand is compact. Shovel spadefuls of wet sand into a mound and pack it down as firmly as you can. As the water in the sand drains away, you will be left with a solid base that you can then carve.

> You can shape the sand with your hands or use tools to carve out finer details. Trowels or plastic knives are good implements for this, but you can use anything – even pieces of driftwood you find on the beach.

> Get the rough shape before you start adding the tiny details as this will help you to visualise the finished sculpture.

> To carve into your sand sculpture, start at the top and work downwards. As you carve, bits of sand will fall away, so by working from the top down you won't have sand falling on bits that you've already finished.

In every out-thrust headland, in every curving beach, in every grain of sand there is the story of the Earth.

RACHEL CARSON

ROCK-POOLING

You don't have to dive beneath the waves to explore our world's underwater kingdom, nor do you have to go to an aquarium. Rock pools are a natural glimpse into this secret world – a microcosm of the sea floor that you can enjoy from the dry land in the fresh sea air.

Also known as tide pools, these pockets of water are located on rocky seafronts around the world, appearing only at low tide when the sea is out, before being subsumed back into the great oceans. They have long fascinated marine biologists with their unique ecosystems and the high adaptability shown by the few organisms that can live there – they must survive being exposed to the sun and wind, the water loss and wave action, not to mention exposure to predators when the tide is out. When they are revealed on the shore, they make for fascinating places where it's easy to discover a wide array of species.

TOP TIPS FOR ROCK-POOLING

> The best time for rock-pooling is low tide on a calm day, when the surface of the pools won't be disturbed by wind and rain. This makes it much easier to see into the water. Check the tide times before you set out as well.

> The most interesting rock-pooling spots – the ones with the most visible sea life – will be the pools closest to the sea's edge. Pools that are further up the beach will often be a mixture of freshwater and seawater, so aren't as habitable for marine life.

> Sturdy footwear with good grip is a must for rock-pooling, as the wet rocks are usually slippery.

> Bring a clear bucket or plastic container with you if you want to take a closer look at the marine life (don't use a net as this can cause damage). Gently dip your container into the pool and leave it until something swims in. Take the container from the water and admire your catch for a short time, but be sure to put everything back where you found it.

> If you can't see anything in the pool at first glance, don't assume that there is nothing there. Look to see if there are patterns in the sand at the bottom of the pool – this could show that there's something hiding just beneath the surface. Sea creatures also tend towards the shadier, sheltered spots, so don't be afraid to turn over rocks and seaweed to see if anything is living underneath. As long as you're gentle and replace everything, you won't cause any harm.

It is advisable to look from the
tide pool to the stars and then
back to the tide pool again.

JOHN STEINBECK

LIVE FREE

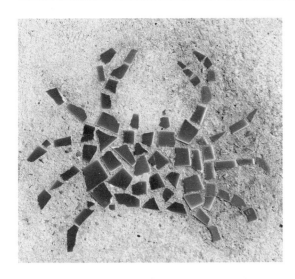

BEACH BARBECUES

A beach barbecue is al fresco dining at its best, mixing the comforts of home with the joy of being outdoors. Nothing beats the simple pleasure of spending a long afternoon on the beach, with the sun on your face, the sand between your toes, the sound of the sea all around, the delicious smell of grilled food on the fresh, seaside breeze and nothing to do except enjoy the time however you want.

Play games on the beach as you wait for the food to cook, catch up and reminisce with old friends, or simply sit and gaze out at the ocean together. The simple act of feeling awe, as we experience when we look at the sea, causes the brain to release chemicals that make us feel connected to the universe. They also make us feel more deeply connected to the people around us, so sharing this moment with friends strengthens your bond and makes your trip to the beach the time out that you need to refresh and recharge.

TOP TIPS FOR BARBECUES

> Some beaches have restrictions about when and where you are allowed to barbecue, so make sure to check these before you go.

> Use a disposable barbecue or invest in a portable, reusable one.

> Keep uncooked foods in a cooler, and bring a bin bag or two to make the clean-up easier at the end.

> Arrange your coals in the barbecue to get a range of heats on your grill. Thinner foods, like bacon, can be cooked on the higher heats (i.e. directly over the coals), and things that need longer can cook more gently with indirect heat (i.e. few or no coals underneath).

> Extinguish disposable barbecues carefully. Pour plenty of water and sand on to the coals to put out any remaining embers. Then let it cool down completely before moving it – this may take a couple of hours. Even once the barbecue has been moved, do not walk on the sand beneath it, as this will still be hot and could burn.

GARLIC HASSELBACK POTATOES Serves 4

INGREDIENTS

4 medium-sized jacket
   potatoes
Butter or olive oil
Salt and pepper, to taste
8 garlic cloves
1 onion, thinly sliced

Optional: cheese; herbs,
such as thyme or rosemary

METHOD

First, prick holes in the skins of each of your potatoes using a fork. Then cut slits in the top of each one about halfway down into the potato.

Rub olive oil, salt and pepper over the outsides of each potato and place on a piece of foil. Place a whole garlic clove in the slit closest to the centre of the potato, and use an extra garlic clove per potato, thinly sliced, to fill the other slits.

Add a thin slice of onion to each slit, then add a drizzle of olive oil or a dab of butter to each.

Wrap the foil tightly around each potato and place at the bottom of your BBQ grill for 1 hour, or until soft. Serve with your favourite toppings.

SEA KAYAKING

>>>————————————————————➤

A kayak may be small – you could even say they look unassuming compared to larger vessels, such as dinghies and yachts – but don't be fooled by appearances. In its minimal design, thousands of years of history and skill are condensed. First used by the Inuit and Aleut people over 4,000 years ago, kayaks are narrow vessels big enough for only one or two people, which can be paddled on rivers, lakes and seas. Though small, they are agile and durable, which has enabled people to travel incredible distances in them – one of the longest kayak journeys ever recorded being a 30,000-mile trip from Germany to Australia which took seven and a half years, from 1932 to 1939.

Kayaking brings you closer to the water than perhaps any other sport, short of swimming. Hunkered down at the waterline, you glide along, feeling the dip and swell of every wave. If you're paddling on a calmer day, out on the open water, you have a unique opportunity to enjoy the scenery and watch the local wildlife go by. However, if the water is choppier, sea kayaking can be intense exercise for your arms and core as you will be paddling against the waves, making it great for improving your overall fitness level.

Whatever the conditions, deep breaths of sea air do wonders for the body and your sense of well-being. The salty air helps to clear your lungs, and it's also naturally abundant in negatively charged ions. These ions can neutralise damaging free radicals (positive ions) that occur in the body, which keeps your cells healthy, and they can also help to increase levels of serotonin, the happy hormone, giving you a mood boost and a greater sense of calm.

If you fancy testing your strength against the waves, there are many organisations that provide courses and trips for beginners and experienced kayakers alike.

The ocean stirs the heart,
inspires the imagination and
brings eternal joy to the soul.

ROBERT WYLAND

SEA SAILING

>>> ————————————————►

The power of nature is seldom more apparent than when you're slicing through the water on a dinghy, the wind in your hair and spray flying up all around you. When you're sailing, that power is right there in your hands, and with just a pull of a rope and a nudge of the rudder, you can harness the energy of the wind and reach exhilarating speeds.

Of course, not all sailing experiences are so adrenaline-fuelled – sailing can also be an incredibly calming pursuit. A smooth trip over calm waters can be just as rewarding as a high-speed dash through the waves. When the sea is still, sailing can be almost meditative, with no sound but the gentle creak of the hull, the ripple of the sail, the soft stream of water against the boat, and the distant call of gulls and the sounds from the shore.

The joy of sailing is something that everybody can enjoy, no matter what their ability. If you're looking for a place to start, many clubs offer taster sessions, or you can pay for a more intensive course at various activity centres, so even if you've never set foot on a boat before, there are plenty of opportunities to get out on the water.

LET THE SEA SET YOU FREE

So throw off the bowlines. Sail away from the safe harbour. Catch the trade winds in your sails. Explore. Dream. Discover.

SARAH FRANCES BROWN

COASTEERING

>>> ————————————————▶

Coasteering is a true adventure, and one of the most immersive ways to enjoy the coast. Essentially it's a natural obstacle course, and involves travelling a route across a coastline, crossing whatever terrain comes your way, be it rocks, water, cliffs or caves.

Compared to activities like sailing and kayaking, which are thousands of years old, coasteering is relatively new to the scene. The first known use of the term was in 1973, and coasteering gained popularity in the 1990s, particularly in the UK, where its rocky coastlines lent themselves to the sport. But despite its newcomer status, enthusiasm for coasteering has soared and there are now hundreds of adventure centres that offer the activity. It's not hard to see why it's so popular: a mixture of swimming, climbing, hiking, scrambling and cliff jumping, coasteering is equal parts exciting, demanding and exhilarating, and it's a way to experience the coast with your whole being.

As it's such a full-body activity, coasteering will challenge your fitness, your strength and your stamina. But, as there are different routes for differing levels of ability, whether you're always active or looking to try something new, there's something for everyone.

The sport is not without its risks and should not be undertaken without the proper gear, including a wetsuit, high-grip shoes, a buoyancy aid and a helmet. You will also need a good knowledge of the terrain and tides of the area. If you go on a trip with an adventure organisation (strongly recommended), they will provide this equipment for you to ensure that you're safe, leaving you free to have the time of your life.

SURFING

>>>————————————————————▶

Surfing is one of the most iconic beach sports there is, and it's a favourite across the world for good reason: there's nothing quite like the natural high of catching a wave.

The best surfers make it look effortless, but the sport requires both strength – particularly in the upper body – and balance. Surfing takes work and patience, and the few seconds spent on the wave might appear to be little pay-off for the time spent overall in the water. But any surfer will tell you that it's worth the effort. When you're riding the crest of the wave there's no room for anything but the present. For a few seconds, your whole attention is on the water and you're at one with the sea as you glide on the top of the wave towards the beach – balance, strength, timing and anticipation all combine in that one instant to create a sense of sheer joy. It's intoxicating and thrilling, and after you've done it once, you'll be back again and again.

If you've never picked up a board, take a surfing lesson or two and learn how to read the waves and catch them like a pro. Not only will this ensure that you're surfing safely, but your skills will improve much faster with expert advice, and you'll be riding the waves in no time.

Surf etiquette

There's no referee in the surfing community, but there is a strict code of conduct. Knowing the etiquette will save you from embarrassment and keep you and your fellow wave-cravers safe.

> **Hang on to your board:** Even if you have a leash, never let go of your board, as when it slips away it could easily hit other people in the water.

> **Stick to waves you can handle:** Stay in the shallower water if you're starting out, and save trying out bigger waves for when you're more confident. This way you'll catch more waves and you're less likely to get in the way of fellow surfers.

> **Keep an eye out:** Watch out for other surfers in the water, make sure your route is clear before catching a wave, and be mindful of others behind you.

> **Paddle around:** When paddling out to a wave, paddle around the break rather than through it so as to avoid other surfers.

> **Don't drop in:** In other words, don't try to overtake someone and catch a wave that they are already riding. Not only is it rude, it's dangerous too.

WiNDSURFiNG

The joy of surfing and the skill of sailing come together in this thrilling water sport. Like surfing, the sailor rides atop a lightweight board, and like sailing, the vessel is controlled by angling a large sail against the wind. Different to both, however, is that the agility and light weight of the board and sail allow for an element of freestyle, meaning that experienced sailors can perform jumps and spins and loops as they go. Flying across the water, with nothing but the sound of the wind and the sea in your ears, windsurfing is a rush, and a release from the everyday.

Balance and core strength are the key skills that you'll need for this sport, and an hour on the water will give you a full-body workout. But, wrapped in the excitement of the moment and the urge to catch the next gust of wind in your sails, it's not a workout you'll even realise you're doing. Spending time in the sea has many health benefits too; rich in salt and magnesium, sea water can help your body to heal, and to keep your muscles, blood and metabolism healthy.

Unless you're experienced and already have your own board, consider taking a few lessons to try your hand at the sport and to be sure that you're practising on the right kind of equipment. Although windsurfing is classed as an extreme sport, it only becomes extreme once you've reached a certain skill level – starting out is relatively safe, which is perfect for those who are looking for an adrenaline rush without too much risk. Once you've felt the sense of adventure and freedom that windsurfing can give you, you'll be hooked.

LIVE
IN THE
SUNSHINE,
SWIM
THE SEA,
DRINK
THE
WILD AIR'S
SALUBRITY.

RALPH WALDO EMERSON

SEASHELLS

>>>───────────────────────────────▶

When you go to the beach and come across a beautiful shell, if you feel the urge to pick it up, admire it and keep it, you're taking part in a practice that's thousands of years old. Across the ages, and in all parts of the world, human beings have always collected shells. They are one of nature's most fascinating and mysterious treasures – they are the jewels of the sea.

Every shell that you see on the beach once belonged to something living. Its previous owner could have died and decomposed, such as a sea snail, or it could have discarded the shell when it outgrew it, like a hermit crab. The sea floor is littered with these beautiful remains, and when they wash up on the shore we can enjoy them too.

Their beauty has seen them being used in jewellery, art and even as a form of currency in some West African cultures. The strength and varying shapes of shells has led to them being used as tools, such as bowls, oil lamps and blades.

Look out for these kinds of shells:

Clam

Conch

Cerith

Mussel

Moon shell

Cockle

Limpet

Note: As tempting as it is to gather all the shells you see, it's important to consider how your actions could have an impact on the ecosystem. Taking one or two shells as a memento of your trip isn't likely to do harm, but the more a beach is combed for shells, the fewer there are available to the plants and animals that depend on them to live. An afternoon spent finding and identifying shells is just as enjoyable as collecting shells to take home, and it's much better for the environment if you put them back where you found them.

FiNDiNG CRABS

There are over 44,000 different species in the crustacean family, but perhaps one of the most well known is the humble crab, which inhabits beaches and oceans the world over and has around 4,500 species to its name. The smallest, at only a couple of centimetres across, is the pea crab, and the largest is the Japanese spider crab, which can easily have a leg span of around 4 metres.

Crustaceans are characterised by their hard exoskeleton, which is moulted whenever the creature inside outgrows it. This is why you're likely to find discarded crab shells as you walk along the beach. These are fascinating enough in themselves, and give you a close-up look at what these intriguing creatures (and their notorious pincers) look like. But for those who aren't squeamish it's possible to get an even more exciting look at these crustaceans.

If you're on a sandy beach, you can search for sand crabs – also known as ghost, white or mole crabs. This sand-dwelling species is small, between 5 and 7.5 centimetres long, and the easiest place to find them is at the waterline. Stand in the shallows of the breaking waves and scoop out a small hole in the sand that's deep enough for you to submerge your hand. When the next wave comes in and the hole fills with water, gently dig a little more with your fingers – your efforts are likely to reward you

with a sand crab. When the wave pulls back, the crab will be held in your tiny pool. If you want to take a closer look, use both hands to scoop it up, being careful not to crush it as you do. Once you've admired it, release it back into the sea and watch it burrow down into the sand.

If you want an encounter with larger species, look up crabbing spots in your local area. Using string with bait attached to the end, such as chicken or bacon, you can lure out larger crabs from rocky coastlines or quaysides. Simply let your baited line drop into the rock-strewn shallows, and wait until you feel a bite. Bring the string up slowly and transfer your crab to a bucket filled with seaweed and small stones (making sure to return them to the sea afterwards).

How to hold a crab:

Hold crabs with your finger and thumb just below the base of the pincers. This way, they won't be able to pinch you!

SEABIRD WATCHING

When you think of a trip to the beach or seafront, you'll probably imagine the sound of the waves crashing against the shore, perhaps the clatter and clang of sails on boats in the harbour, and seabirds calling in the skies. Birds are all around us, and never more so than by the sea, which is home to almost 350 species of seabird, spread across practically every corner of the globe.

With their webbed feet which help them get around both on land and in water, and their swooping flight and sudden dives, they're easy to spot and often striking to look at – especially the huge albatross (with a wingspan of up to 3.5 metres), the comical-looking puffin, and the stately frigatebird with its hooked bill and pointed tail and wings. They are well adapted to life at sea, with built-in sunglasses to help with the glare from the water, and special salt glands which filter the salt from seawater and fish and excrete it through their nostrils.

They are truly amazing creatures, and beautiful when in flight. You can while away hours watching these magnificent birds wheel and swoop in and around each other. Look up the species of seabird near you – gannets, terns, cormorants or gulls – and seek out spots where they're likely to make an appearance. Equally enjoyable is taking a set of binoculars to the beach to simply wait and see what comes along, seabird or otherwise, enjoying the time spent out in the fresh air, absorbing the landscape and the rich wildlife that surrounds you.

How inappropriate to call
this planet Earth when
it is clearly Ocean.

ARTHUR C. CLARKE

Seaside treasures: mussels

With their deep blue-black shells, mussels are one of the most distinctive shellfish, and a delicacy in many coastal regions. They also have the advantage of being both recognisable and abundant, so if you're new to foraging they make a great place to start. High in iron, calcium and omega-3, mussels are not only a delicious souvenir from your trip to the beach, but a healthy boost for your blood cells and bones too.

Mussels can be found most easily on rocky shores, but you can also hunt for them on jetties or even on the hulls of boats. Look for shiny, firmly closed mussels and only pick a few from each area so as not to eradicate an entire colony. For the best flavour, look for mid-sized mussels. Lots will be easily harvested by simply twisting and pulling them, but you can come prepared with a pocketknife to cut away the beard on any tough ones.

You may have heard that harvesting mussels is dangerous, but it's perfectly safe as long as the right precautions are taken. Folklore says that they should only be collected during months that have an 'r' in them, i.e. any time other than May, June, July and August – and there's wisdom in this. During these summer months, hotter weather means that seawater often has higher levels of bacteria so it's not as safe to forage then. You should also make sure that your foraging area does not have high levels of water algae, that you are away from human habitation, and that you're not foraging during a 'red tide', where particular kinds of algae stain the water red, opening seafood to the risk of contamination.

THAi-STYLE STEAMED MUSSELS Serves 2

METHOD

As soon as you arrive home with your foraged mussels, soak them overnight in a bowl of cold salted water so that they filter themselves clean of grit. Discard any mussels that have opened.

Finely slice the onion and garlic. Heat oil in a large, lidded pan and cook the onion and garlic on a low heat until softened.

Remove the woody outer layers from the lemongrass and finely chop. Then slice the chilli and grate the ginger. Add these to the pan, along with the coconut milk, coconut cream, coriander (leaves and stalks), fish sauce, curry paste and lime zest. Stir to incorporate and until the coconut cream has dissolved.

Bring to the boil, then add the mussels. Cover and cook for 5 minutes, or until the mussels have opened. Once cooked, discard any that remain closed.

Serve with the lime juice and a sprinkling of fresh coriander leaves and spring onion, if desired.

INGREDIENTS

1 kg mussels
1 small white onion
2 cloves garlic
1 tbsp oil
1 stem lemongrass
1 red chilli
3 cm ginger
200 ml coconut milk
40 ml coconut cream
½ bunch fresh coriander,
   plus extra for garnish
1 tsp fish sauce
½ tbsp Thai green
   curry paste
Juice and zest of 1 lime
Chopped spring onion,
   to serve

Seaside treasures: laver

Laver is a species of seaweed that grows in cold, shallow seawater. Different species are eaten all over the world, including nori, which is used in Japan to wrap sushi. The plant grows as a purple-green sheet and is sometimes described as looking like a bin bag, but don't be put off by the comparison. Laver is a wonderful flavouring ingredient which goes well with most vegetable-based dishes. It will give your stir-fries, soups, stews, fried rice, pasta and noodle dishes a delicious savoury quality.

Due to its time spent in the ocean, seaweed has a higher mineral content than any other vegetable, which means there are many health benefits associated with it. Laver in particular has a high content of calcium, iron and vitamin B12, which means it's excellent for promoting healthy blood cells. As with many seaweeds, laver is also a good source of iodine, which, among other things, contributes to maintaining your metabolism.

Laver is abundant between November and May, and can be found on exposed rocks that lie roughly in the middle of the tidal range. To harvest, clip away pieces of the laver sheets rather than pulling whole sheets off the rock. This means that the plant will be able to regrow and replenish itself much faster. Store it in a bucket or plastic container until you return home.

VEGETABLE EGG-FRIED RICE WITH TOASTED LAVER Serves 4

INGREDIENTS

50 g laver
1 tbsp sesame oil
1 large onion, sliced
80 g peas
2 red peppers, sliced
3 garlic cloves, crushed
300 g brown rice, cooked
2 tbsp dark soy sauce
1 egg, whisked
Sesame seeds, to garnish
   (optional)

METHOD

Thoroughly rinse the laver, then put it in a large pan, cover it with water and simmer on a low heat with the lid on for 6 hours. Check on the pan periodically to make sure it doesn't boil dry and add more water as necessary.

Drain the seaweed (retaining the liquid if you like, as this makes an excellent vegetable stock for soups and stews) and squeeze until dry.

Preheat the oven to 200°C/390°F/gas mark 6. Put the laver on to a baking tray and roast in the oven for 5 minutes, or until it is crisp to the touch. Remove from the oven, break into small pieces and put to one side.

Heat a wok or large frying pan and add the oil. Once the oil is hot, add the chopped vegetables, garlic and one tablespoon of the soy sauce. Cook on a high heat for 4 minutes, keeping the vegetables moving all the time.

Add the cooked rice and laver and cook for a further minute. Make a space in the pan and pour over the whisked egg. Once it's half cooked, mix it in with the rice and vegetables. Then add the remaining soy sauce.

Season to taste and serve immediately, sprinkling each serving with sesame seeds if you wish.

the voice OF THE SEA SPEAKS to the soul

LAKES
& RIVERS

Lakes can be as large as seas or small, calm and pond-like; rivers slowly wend or rush and tumble their course through the landscape. Since prehistory, the movement of these bodies of freshwater has informed every aspect of how we live, and even today our world is built around our waterways. When we get out of the city, we have the chance to appreciate them for the wonders that they are.

RAFT BUILDING

>>>———————————————➤

Whether you want to challenge your construction skills or channel your inner intrepid explorer, raft building is a fun way to spend an afternoon. Enjoy a leisurely paddle on the lake, or race across the water as fast as you can go.

Even though raft building is one of the simplest watercraft activities there is, it takes skill and know-how to make a raft that's seaworthy (or at least lake-worthy!). Modern rafts tend to be inflatable and made from various fabrics or plastics, or they are constructed using barrels to help keep them afloat. But the earliest rafts were made from bundles of reeds or from wood, and this strong and sturdy design is the one that this raft is modelled on.

TOP TIPS FOR RAFT BUILDING

> First, you need to collect your logs or sticks of bamboo, and some lengths of rope. The size of your raft will naturally depend on how many logs you have and how big they are, but don't worry – even a tiny raft will float (you might just have to make do with floating a leaf on the lake, rather than yourself). Try to find dead wood for this as it will float better than green wood. Most types of wood will work, but avoid porous wood if possible. The sticks or logs should be straight and roughly equal in circumference.

> If you want to reuse your raft, you should varnish the wood and leave to dry before putting it in the water, to avoid it soaking up too much moisture and rotting.

> It's best to construct the raft near the water's edge, to avoid having to carry the finished product far, as it will be heavy. Lay your logs down next to each other and tie one end of your rope around the end of the first log, securing with a knot. Then use the rope to bind the logs together, wrapping the rope around the end of each log several times and around the whole structure twice. Make sure to pull the rope tight at all times and tie knots where you feel it could do with extra strength.

> Lay an extra log on top of the raft at each end, at right angles to the base logs, to strengthen the structure. Add one in the middle too if your raft is long. Wrap the rope around between the individual base logs and criss-cross for extra security.

> Test the raft carefully first in shallow water to make sure it floats. Then find yourself a long stick to use as a paddle, and off you go…

FiSHiNG

>>>————————————————————————>

The wonder of fishing is something that more and more people are discovering. As a sport it's always had a reputation for tranquillity (except perhaps when you lose a great catch!), but due to the mood-boosting effects of sunshine and spending time in nature, fishing has now been proven to have emotional benefits too.

Unlike many outdoor activities where you can track your progress or your speed, there's very little that technology can do to improve your experience of fishing. Spending time at the water's edge, waiting patiently for that gentle twitch of rod or float, is a pure and simple break from the modern world, allowing you to slow down and find calm. Just like the float, sitting serenely in the water, your thoughts will also be at rest.

Doubt not but angling will prove to be so pleasant that it will prove to be, like virtue, a reward to itself.

IZAAK WALTON

TOP TIPS FOR FISHING

> Choose your spot: Choosing the right spot is key to having a fulfilling fishing experience: if you're fishing in the wrong place you'll never get a bite, no matter how patient you are. Ask the local tackle shop if they have recommendations, as they'll have expert knowledge of the surrounding area and be keen to share it with you.

> Pick your moment: Fish are most active very early in the morning or at sunset, so for the best fishing sessions be prepared for some early starts or late nights.

> Be aware of the rules: Most lakes, rivers and pools have regulations about who can fish and when. You may need a licence or a day permit, or you may be restricted to certain areas or times. Make sure you're familiar with the rules of your spot before you go to avoid being caught out.

> Take the bait: Not all fish like the same kind of food, so ensure that you've got the right bait on the end of your line. Research the kinds of fish that live where you'll be fishing to make sure you have the tastiest morsels to lure them out with. Natural bait options include worms or maggots, but there is also the option of using artificial baits.

> Think like a fish: It can help to cast your line into shady spots, and anywhere where there's underwater greenery or an assortment of rocks. Fish like to hide, so by looking for them in these areas and bringing the food to them, rather than waiting for them to swim out into the open, you're much more likely to get a bite.

WILD
SWIMMING

>>>————————————▶

Wild swimming is, simply, swimming outdoors, and it is everything you enjoy about your local leisure pool but with a difference.

Wild swimming is about much more than swimming lengths. It's about reconnecting with nature and getting the most out of being in the open. It's a full-body experience of the natural world that involves all of your senses, and, because the natural world is unique every day, no two swims are ever the same.

There are many health benefits to swimming, all of which are enhanced by venturing out into the open air rather than swimming indoors. Not only does it improve your fitness, but the cold water invigorates you, and embracing the chill can even be the source of a natural high. Swimming outdoors and engaging with nature as you swim has also been shown to improve your mood and alleviate feelings of depression.

Another benefit is that it's a low-cost activity. The simple, wholesome pleasure is open to anyone and everyone. If it becomes something you love, it could take you all over the world in search of ever more beautiful locations to swim in.

TOP TIPS FOR WILD SWIMMING

> Know your ability: it sounds obvious, but before you embark on a wild-swimming adventure, make sure that you are proficient at swimming. If you're unsure, ask a lifeguard at your local pool for advice, and the first time you swim in the open ensure that you take it slowly. You don't have to push yourself to enjoy the benefits of the water.

> Always swim with a buddy if you can, or at the very least make sure that someone knows where you're going and when you expect to return. Alternatively, notify someone on the shore that you're swimming so they can watch out for you.

> Never jump into the water if you don't know how deep it is, as this could cause serious injury. If it is safe to jump, acclimatise your body to the water temperature by paddling or dangling your feet in first to prevent your body from going into shock.

> Cover any cuts before you get in, try not to swallow any water and shower thoroughly once you've finished swimming. It's very unlikely that you will catch an illness from wild swimming, but minimising the risk is always best practice.

> If you're worried about the cold, invest in a wetsuit – or wetsuit boots and gloves and a swimming cap – to keep your extremities warmer.

> Always swim around the edge of the lake rather than across the middle. This way, if there is a problem you'll be closer to help.

> Always research before you swim. Are there any regulations to follow? Is it private property? Are there any tides or currents to be aware of? Are there any rocky areas to watch out for? Where is it safe to enter and leave the lake or river?

A lake carries you into recesses of feeling otherwise impenetrable.

WILLIAM WORDSWORTH

GORGE WALKING

>>>————————————▶

A gorge or canyon is a valley that's been carved into the landscape by a stream or river – and they are arguably one of Earth's most stunning geographical features. Some gorges are large enough to be seen from space, such as the Grand Canyon, and these natural phenomena are often thousands if not millions of years old. Others are smaller, and make the perfect setting for a gorge-walking adventure.

Gorge walking is just what it sounds like – exploring a gorge on foot by walking along it. This may sound tame, but the river or stream that carved out the gorge is usually still flowing freely. So as well as walking, you will likely also be swimming, climbing, sliding and scrambling, and navigating waterfalls, rock pools and rapids as you make your way along.

Progress through a gorge will be steady, but it's still an activity to make your heart race with adrenaline as you scramble over rocks, slide down rapids and jump into plunge pools. You're almost guaranteed to be drenched from head to foot by the time you emerge at the other end, but not without a heady sense of glee at what you and your fellow gorge walkers have achieved.

Since you'll be travelling at a steady pace, gorge walking can be enjoyed by people of all experience and fitness levels. Unless you are extremely experienced, it's not recommended to partake in this activity unsupervised. Led by instructors who will be able to provide you with the right equipment – such as a wetsuit, buoyancy aid and a helmet – you can wade up the river safely and securely, free to enjoy the dramatic natural landscape from an entirely unique perspective.

KAYAKING

Kayaking on a river is a completely different adventure to kayaking on the sea. On the sea, you're powering the kayak, whereas on the river the water takes more control. You can use the flow of the river to make kayaking what you want it to be.

You can choose to have a more leisurely trip, letting the flow of the river carry you downstream. The gentle progress will allow you to enjoy beautiful scenery that you couldn't see from anywhere else, such as gorges and waterfalls. If you're kayaking with a guide, they'll be able to tell you more about the area you're travelling through, from the plants and wildlife to the local stories and legends. Despite the river flow guiding the kayak, it is still a good workout: the paddling motion that you need to steer and control the kayak works your arms and torso, and the posture required helps to improve your balance.

If you're looking for adventure, you can take to the rapids and rush along the river at top speed. This activity will really put your strength to the test, as your control of the boat relies on your arms and your core. But when you're in the moment, you won't notice the workout – with the water roaring in your ears and the foam flying, you'll feel exhilarated as you steer your tiny boat over and around the rapids. There's no time to think about anything other than the wild water and the boat. It's such an extreme break from the pace of everyday life, you'll emerge at the other end feeling energised and ready for more.

Whatever your level of experience on the water, there will be something for you. There are plenty of centres that allow you to rent kayaks for a day, or if you want to experience the white water, join a trip where an experienced kayaker can guide you through it.

If there is magic on this planet,
it is contained in water.

LOREN EISELEY

LAKE SAILING

You don't have to be close to the sea to experience the joy of sailing – lakes of all shapes and sizes give you the opportunity to take to the water even if you are inland.

There are a few notable differences between sailing on a lake and sailing on the sea. One is that the wind tends to be more changeable on lakes. It may suddenly drop, or you could experience sudden strong gusts that sweep you along. These quick-changing conditions can make lake sailing particularly exciting, with the added bonus of giving you plenty of practice at adjusting your sails to the conditions.

Sailing on lakes, especially smaller ones, presents more opportunities to practise manoeuvres such as tacking (moving in a zigzag pattern). This essential sailing move comes in handy on a lake where you'll need to change course often to avoid running aground.

However, although there are slight differences between lake and sea sailing, what doesn't change is the essence of the sport itself. On the deck of your boat you'll still have the breeze in your hair, the sun on your face and the inimitable feeling of racing through the water with the power of the wind in your own two hands.

A lake is the landscape's most beautiful and expressive feature. It is Earth's eye; looking into which the beholder measures the depth of his own nature.

HENRY DAVID THOREAU

PADDLEBOARDING

Despite its prevalence as a modern water sport, paddleboarding or SUPing (stand-up paddleboarding) has been around for thousands of years, and has been practised by cultures all over the world.

It's simple and minimal – instead of countless items of equipment, all you need is a board and a paddle and you're ready to go. In addition to rigid boards, there are many inflatable versions on the market, which means you can easily transport your vessel to the water. If you paddle with friends it can be a social event, but you can also go alone, and those who do find that it's one of the most meditative sports there is.

Paddleboarding requires the sailor to remain still, centred, steady and calm, so it's not only a fantastic activity to strengthen your core and improve your balance, but it's also a calming experience. It forces you to slow down, and – as being rigid will only make you fall – it helps you to find a position of both stillness and relaxation within your own body as you gaze out into the horizon. Out on the water, feeling calm and strong, you can let your worries go, clear your mind and recharge.

Make your heart like a lake, with a calm, still surface, and great depths of kindness.

LAO TZU

ROWING

If you're looking to unwind, while away a leisurely afternoon in a rowing boat. What could be more relaxing than gliding through the water, the gentle creak of oars against the side of the boat, admiring the flora and fauna as you float by, and listening to the soft splash of the paddles and the lapping of water against the riverbank?

RiVER DiPPiNG

Have you ever stood on the bank of a river or stream and peered into the water? If it's shallow, the water is often clear; you can see the stones on the riverbed and the soft swaying of the underwater grasses as they're pulled by the current. The longer you look, the more you see: the details of the plants, perhaps tiny insects on the surface of the water, or even some fish.

Rivers are bursting with wildlife of all shapes and sizes, and all you need to do is take the time to notice it. River dipping is the perfect way to do this, and spending an hour or so getting to know the wildlife that's in your area is not only rewarding, but it's a chance to connect with nature that we don't often encounter.

River dipping can rekindle our sense of wonder at the natural world; it is a reminder that rivers are not merely stretches of running water. They are vast and complex ecosystems, and home to creatures that have evolved for millions of years to adapt to this exact environment and place. It reminds us that awe can be found anywhere and everywhere you look in the great outdoors, from the top of the highest mountains, to the smallest shallows of our rivers.

TOP TIPS FOR RIVER DIPPING

> The best time of year for river dipping is between May and August, as this is when the river wildlife will be at its most active and abundant.

> The essential equipment is a net and a tray or large jar. You might also want to bring a spoon so you can look at your findings more closely, or even a magnifying glass. If you're keen to identify the species you find, pack a field guide as well.

> Bring a camera to record your findings and to remember the occasion by!

> Keep noise levels low as many creatures are sensitive to sound. The quieter you are and the slower you move, the more likely you are to see wildlife.

> Before you scoop anything from the river with the net, fill the tray/jar with river water. When you do find something, you'll be able to lift it straight from the river and into the tray, causing minimal distress.

> When using the net, lower it gently into the river. Hold it still and let the water run through it. Gently lift it from the water and transfer the contents immediately into your prepared tray of water and see what you've found.

> If you're not having any luck, try holding your net in different areas of the river, or moving it slowly in a figure-of-eight motion to increase your chances. You could even wade in a little way to reach a different spot. If you're patient you're bound to discover something!

> When you're admiring the creatures you've found, resist the urge to touch them – this will keep the creatures happier, and you safe from the potential threat of being bitten.

> When you've finished, make sure you return everything to the river where you found it.

When you put your hand in a flowing stream, you touch the last that has gone before and the first of what is still to come.

LEONARDO DA VINCI

River treasures: crayfish

Crayfish are crustaceans which can be found in freshwater. Looking like tiny lobsters, these small creatures inhabit rivers, ponds, lakes and marshes the world over. They go by many names, including crawfish, crawdads, freshwater lobsters, mudbugs and yabbies.

The body and claws are edible, but the crayfish tails are the most commonly used part and are an ingredient for all manner of dishes, from soups and stews to pastas, barbecues and seafood platters. They are a source of low-fat protein and full of vitamins and minerals, including B vitamins which help to maintain a healthy metabolism and contribute to healthy skin, eyes and hair, so crayfish are not only delicious but a beneficial addition to your diet.

Before you go foraging for crayfish, you will need to do some research into the local populations. For instance, in the UK, the native white-clawed crayfish is endangered by an invasive species, the signal crayfish. Foraging for signal crayfish is therefore encouraged as it helps to restore the white-clawed crayfish population. This also means that foragers should check their catch carefully – if any white-clawed crayfish have bitten the line, they should be released back into the wild. If you're fishing outside the UK, ensure that you abide by that country's fishing and foraging regulations.

Once you've picked an area to forage in, prepare a baited line, like you would for crabbing. Crayfish will be attracted to a variety of things, including an old fish head or a piece of bacon. When you feel a bite, gently lift your line to see what you've caught! Place your catch into a high-sided bucket, and release any by-catch back into the water.

HOW TO PREPARE CRAYFISH TAILS

Sort through your catch, discarding any that have already died.

Place your crayfish in the freezer and chill them to between 2°C and 4°C, which takes approximately 10 minutes. Once they have reached this temperature, kill them immediately with a sharp knife, either between the eyes or through the chest, to minimise distress.

Take a pan large enough to hold your crayfish catch and fill it two-thirds full with water. Season with a tablespoon of salt and bring to the boil.

Add the crayfish to the pan and boil them for 5 minutes, or until they have turned bright red.

Remove from the pan and leave to cool. Twist off the tails and crack them open to remove the meat.

CRAYFISH AND MUSHROOM RISOTTO Serves 2

>>> ⟶

INGREDIENTS

1 tbsp olive oil
1 small onion, chopped
2 garlic cloves, crushed
120 g mushrooms, sliced
150 g Arborio rice
90 ml white wine
Zest of 1 lemon
500 ml chicken, fish or
  vegetable stock
100 g crayfish tail meat
  (approx. 7 crayfish)
50 g Parmesan
50 ml double cream
Handful chives, chopped

METHOD

In a deep frying pan, heat the oil and add the onion and garlic. Fry on a medium heat until soft.

Then add the mushrooms and continue to cook for another 5 minutes, stirring occasionally.

Add the rice and stir for a minute, then add the wine and lemon zest. Stir gently until the liquid has been absorbed.

Then add a small amount of the stock. Stir continuously until the stock has been absorbed, then add another small amount. Continue until all the stock has been absorbed, then stir in the crayfish. Stir until heated through.

Take the pan off the heat and stir in the Parmesan, double cream and half the chives. Stir until well incorporated.

Serve topped with the remaining chives.

River treasures: water mint

Water mint, or *Mentha aquatica* as it is sometimes known, is a member of the mint family. As its name suggests, it flourishes in wet ground, and for this reason it can often be found growing around lakes, rivers and ponds. Like the common mint plant, it has leaves with serrated edges, but unlike mint, they are tinged with purple and are deeply veined. It also has distinctive purple flowers; from a distance the plant appears to have one large round flower at the top of its stem, but it is in fact made up of lots of smaller flowers all grouped together.

The edible parts of the water mint plant are its leaves, which have been used in herbal remedies for thousands of years, and with good reason. Mint has been shown to soothe the stomach and promote healthy digestion, to ease feelings of nausea and to reduce inflammation. It's a simple but refreshing herb, and grows abundantly.

Water mint is perennial, so the leaves can be harvested at any time (although you may have more success in warmer months). To collect them, pick a few leaves from plants as you pass, and store them in a breathable bag if you're bringing them home. The youngest leaves have the best flavour, so aim for these if you want a strong minty quality. If you're not using the mint immediately, freeze the leaves then transfer to an airtight container in the freezer, where they will keep for up to three months.

WATER MINT TEA

INGREDIENTS

A handful of water mint
   leaves, fresh or dried
Boiling water

METHOD

If you are using fresh leaves, wash them before use.

Place a few of the leaves in a mug of hot water and leave for a few minutes to brew.

Add sugar to taste, and enjoy a cup of fresh water mint tea.

UPLANDS & LOWLANDS

Uplands and lowlands make up the green spaces of our world, stitching the land together in a patchwork of fields, plains and hills. They are as varied as they are expansive, and to explore them on foot, bike or horseback is a joy that all should have the chance to experience.

HiKiNG AND WALKiNG

Hiking is one of the easiest ways to get out into the fresh air and to make the most of the great outdoors. Whatever you choose to call it – rambling, hillwalking, fell-walking – hiking is, simply, walking, which makes it endlessly adaptable, and something that everybody can try. Walk for an hour or for a whole day, up steep hills or across wide plains, alone or with friends, walk the beaten track or explore beyond it – the world is yours to discover as you walk your way through it.

Many natural spaces can only be reached on foot, so when you hike you're opening yourself up to a whole new world of possibility. On foot, you are free. You are able to walk, stride or wander where you want, discovering your own paths, and experiencing the most stunning views that nature has to offer – views seen by only the dedicated few who take the time to seek them out.

The steady pace of putting one foot in front of the other is calming and grounding, as well as a great cardiovascular workout, and when you're hiking you're relying on your own strength to carry you from point A to B. So when you reach the top of that hill – however tired you are – you can look out at the view before you and see just how far you've come, with the satisfaction of knowing that *you* made it happen.

TOP TIPS FOR HIKING

> Select the right trail for your fitness level. Not only will this keep you safe, but it's the best way to guarantee that you enjoy your walk!

> Bring a map and compass with you, but always check the trail before you go so you have an idea of where you're going.

> Check the weather and pack appropriately, including all the essentials: plenty of water, some snacks, sunscreen, a map, a charged phone, a warm waterproof layer, a jumper and a first-aid kit.

> Invest in some sturdy shoes. They needn't be expensive, but having reliable footwear will keep your feet comfortable and your ankles safe.

> Explore, but stay safe. Although it's usually fine to stray a little way from a trail to take a closer look at something growing, or to explore the area, be mindful of where you are. If signs tell you to stick to the trail, stick to it, as there could be dangers in the surrounding environment.

> Tell someone where you're going and when you expect to be back. If the worst does happen, they can raise the alarm as early as possible.

WiLD CAMPiNG

Wild camping is all about freedom. It's the perfect escape from the bustle of the city and an opportunity to get back to basics and go well and truly wild.

Wild camping is camping anywhere in the outdoors that isn't an official campsite and involves embracing the bare necessities of life. Your shelter and belongings are limited to the things that you're able to carry on your back; unshackled from modern living, you are liberated. Surrounded by the natural world, you can go anywhere, stay anywhere, do anything – there is no greater sense of freedom.

It can be a daunting prospect, as you have to rely completely on yourself and the others in your group. You can't take a quick trip to the toilet block in the middle of the night or buy replacement kit if something breaks. But the challenge and total disconnect from the everyday is a large part of its appeal. There's no agenda, no schedule. You're in charge of your own adventure. Where will the next day take you? It's completely up to you.

As well as the general camping tips which can be found on p.13, here are some extra tips for wild campers:

ADVENTURE IS WORTHWHILE IN ITSELF.

AMELIA EARHART

> Pack as lightly as you can without missing out on the essentials. The lighter your load, the easier it will be to walk, explore and enjoy the outdoors.

> When picking a spot to pitch your tent, aim to find somewhere flat and away from any footpaths or thoroughfares.

> Some places have laws about wild camping, so ensure that you check your area for any regulations before you pitch your tent.

> Take plenty of warm layers, as nights can be cold.

> Invest in, or borrow, a good-quality tent. Ideally it should also be lightweight; for example, a two-person tent would weigh no more than 2 kilograms. These lighter tents are expensive, but the material is of much higher quality.

> Take all your toilet waste back with you. Or, if this is not possible, make sure to bury it at least 15 centimetres underground (and don't bury toilet paper).

EXPLORE MORE

NATURAL NAVIGATION

Navigating using only what is to hand in the natural world is a useful skill as much as it is a fun challenge – many would call it an art form, as it takes dedication and patience to become truly proficient. Below are a few tips to help you orientate yourself in the Northern hemisphere without the assistance of GPS or even a compass, by using the clues around you.

The sun

Most people are familiar with the fact that the sun rises in the east but sets in the west. As a broad indicator of direction, this statement rings true. But if you're looking for an accurate reading of where you are, you will also need to take your position on the Earth and the time of year into account. For instance, in the northern hemisphere the sun rises in the north-east in the summer and the south-east in winter, due to the fact that the Earth tilts on its axis in different ways throughout the year.

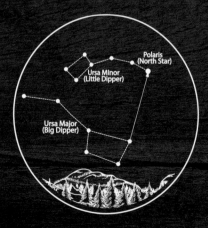

Polaris (North Star)

Ursa Minor (Little Dipper)

Ursa Major (Big Dipper)

Polaris, the North Star

Contrary to popular legend, the North Star is not the brightest star in the night sky – in fact, it's dimmer than some of the surrounding stars – but it's still easy enough to find. First find the Big Dipper constellation. Then look at the two outermost stars of the 'bowl'. Imagine a ruler connecting the two, then follow that line up and you'll find Polaris – true north.

The moon

If there's a crescent moon in the sky, you will be able to establish where south is. Imagine you're matching a ruler against the tip of each crescent. Carry the line straight on to the ground and you will find south. This is only an approximate reading, but it will help to give you more information about your surroundings if you need it.

Rocks

This tip works best during the day. Place your hand on a large rock and feel the temperature of each side. The warmest part of the rock will give you an indication of where the sun is, which will help to find your way on a cloudy day.

Moss

Find a tree that is relatively out in the open and check the trunk for where moss is growing. Whereas trees seek the sun, moss prefers cool, shady places to grow. In other words, the moss-free side will indicate the south, which receives plenty of sunlight, and wherever there is moss on a tree it generally indicates the north.

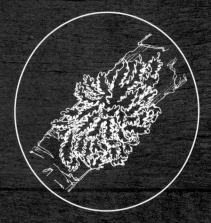

LOOK DEEP INTO NATURE, AND THEN YOU WILL UNDERSTAND EVERYTHING BETTER.

ALBERT EINSTEIN

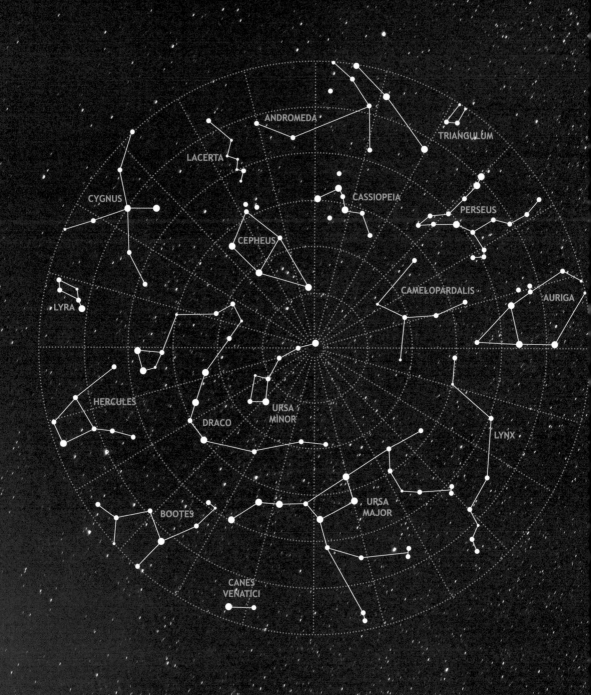

STARGAZING

Stargazing is one of the most magical ways to spend an evening in the outdoors. Find a spot away from the light pollution of cities and towns, spread out a blanket and sit back to enjoy the beautiful show that appears in our night skies.

THE SIGHT OF THE STARS ALWAYS MAKES ME DREAM.

VINCENT VAN GOGH

TRAiL RUNNiNG

>>>———————————————————————————————————►

If you run to clear your head after a long day at work, if you enjoy the steady rhythm of your feet hitting the ground as you move, if you love the high at the end of a run and you feel like you've conquered the world – try trail running for size.

Trail running is the sport of following a trail through a natural landscape. It's everything you love about running but with the added bonus of being out in fresh air with nature all around you. As you're not running on tarmac, it's also slightly softer going on your knees and ankles, which is another benefit of taking to the trails.

While not as extreme as fell running (see p.86), trail running is still a challenging sport as the routes can take you both high and low, and the terrain is as varied as the weather conditions you'll encounter. You could be running over rocky paths, grass or through streams, in rain, sun, cloud and fog. Every trail is different – even the same trail will be unique every time you run it.

As you run you'll not only feel the exhil-aration of movement and the gradual clearing of your mind, but you'll feel excitement and energy as you explore the world around you – trail running puts the sense of adventure back into running.

In the presence of nature, a wild delight runs through the man.

RALPH WALDO EMERSON

TOP TIPS FOR TRAIL RUNNING

> Wear the right shoes. Trail-running shoes have a stronger grip for the terrain and tend to have a lower heel, which helps to protect your ankles.

> Keep your eyes on the trail. Sometimes the path can be narrow and, especially with rocky terrain, you'll need to keep an eye on where to put your feet.

> Consider using trekking poles if your route is steep as they're useful for balance and will help to reduce the impact on your joints.

> Be considerate of your fellow runners. Generally speaking, those running uphill pause for those who are running downhill. If there are puddles, try not to splash if there are people running past!

> Use your arms to help you balance and navigate up and down terrain.

> Be prepared to slow your pace. Trail running is a different skill to road running, and the rapid changes in terrain and gradient can call for slower speeds. If you can make these adjustments as you go, you'll be able to run further.

HORSE RiDiNG AND PONY-TREKKiNG

Pony-trekking and horse riding are somewhere between adventure and relaxation. The steady beat of hoofs beneath you is lulling, but sitting atop a horse or pony you're exploring the world around you from an entirely new perspective. You're at leisure to absorb the scenery, colours and life around you, whether it's a leafy lane, the flora and fauna of a forest or a wide-open expanse of land.

Equine creatures are noble, majestic and peaceful, and there's something incredible about being in such proximity to them, being able to feel every movement of their strong bodies as they walk, the heat from their flanks, and the rise and fall of every breath they take. There's a bond of trust between you and your steed which can provide a huge confidence boost, especially for those of us who don't usually have the opportunity to interact with animals. As a team, you can explore the hills and fields, and as you ride, their sense of calm will transfer to you.

No hour of life is wasted that is spent in the saddle.

WINSTON CHURCHILL

BiRDWATCHiNG

From birds of prey that wheel in the sky to the smaller birds that dwell in the hedgerows, there are birds to be discovered everywhere in the great outdoors, and the uplands and lowlands – brimming with all manner of avian wildlife – are no exception.

Birdwatching can be anything you want it to be. You can go out specifically to look for birds, or you can incorporate it into a hike or a camping trip. If you find it hard to get away, birdwatching is a good excuse to spend time outdoors – a simple pleasure in itself.

Take your binoculars and field guide and venture out to see what you can find. Or, if you're interested in a more focused experience, look up whether there are any sanctuaries or well-known birdwatching spots near you.

Wherever and however you watch them, stories unfold before you as you spend time with birds in their natural habitat. If you're lucky enough to watch them for a long period of time, you may even start to see their personalities shining through. Birdwatching is at its heart an exercise of patience and stillness, and, as such, it lends itself to quiet contemplation. Combined with the benefits of spending time outdoors, surrounded by everything green, windswept and natural, birdwatching is restorative. When you're concentrating on the birds as they dash in and out of a hedge, or circle elegantly overhead, you will find yourself absorbed in the moment.

From Hummingbird to Eagle, the daily existence of every bird is a remote and bewitching mystery.

THOMAS WENTWORTH HIGGINSON

Meadow treasures: dandelions

If you're a keen gardener, you've probably picked them out of your lawn with disdain, and if not, you'll have enjoyed blowing the seeds and watching them dance on the wind. But did you know that dandelions are also a delicacy?

Dandelions are incredibly abundant, which makes them a forager's dream. Even better is that almost the entire plant can be used – leaves, flowers and roots. The leaves make great additions to salads, bringing a sharp, bitter taste to the mix. Alternatively, they can be sautéed in oil and garlic, like other leafy greens, and enjoyed as a side dish. The roots can be used for making a caffeine-free coffee-like drink, and the yellow heads can be fried, baked into bread or made into wine. In fact, the only parts that can't be consumed are the puffy seed heads – the distinctive dandelion clocks.

As dandelions are weeds, the main caution that must be taken while foraging is to avoid areas that may have had weedkiller sprayed on them, such as public grassy verges.

The best time to forage for these delicious plants is from May to October. To harvest, pick a selection of flower heads or leaves depending on what you'd like to make, and store your pickings in a breathable bag until you return home. Generally, it's discouraged to uproot plants for the sake of foraging, because this damages the plant population. However, as dandelions are so abundant, you could use the roots of these if you take them sparingly from land you have permission to forage on.

DANDELION SYRUP Makes approx. one 454 ml jar

METHOD

Remove the stems from the dandelions and as many of the green leaves from the flower as possible. Then rinse the flowers and pat dry.

Put the water in a large pan and add the flowers. Bring to the boil and leave for 1 minute. Then remove the pan from the heat and allow to infuse overnight.

The following day, strain the liquid through a cheesecloth or clean tea towel, squeezing out as much water as you can. Return the liquid to the pan and discard the flowers.

Then add the sugar, lemon zest and juice to the pan, cover and simmer on a low heat for 1 hour. The syrup will thicken further once it has cooled, so don't be alarmed if it appears thin at the end of the simmering time.

Allow to cool to a safe heat, then adjust to taste with sugar and lemon juice. Transfer to a sterile jar and leave to cool completely. It can keep in the fridge for up to a month.

Pour over pancakes, waffles or porridge for a sweet and totally natural treat.

INGREDIENTS

60 dandelion flowers (approx.)
400 ml water
190 g brown sugar
190 g caster sugar
Juice and zest of half a lemon

Meadow treasures: blackberries

Blackberries are perhaps one of the most recognisable berries there are, and many of us will have memories of long summer afternoons spent searching for these treasures, involving sticky, purple-stained fingers and the delicious, tangy juice running down our chins.

Growing in clumps on thorny stems, blackberries are the reward for those who persevere through the brambles. The best time to look for them is from mid- to late summer (around June to late August), and the bushes are easily identifiable as they form thick briar patches with canes that arch over onto the ground, laden with blackberries.

Collect the berries in any receptacle (a washable plastic box or metal colander works well) by picking them straight off the branch. Due to the brambles, you might want to go armed with gloves, and possibly a long pole or hooked stick to bring the highest branches within reach.

Note: Blackberries sometimes grow near roadsides. Be wary of picking these as they may have been sprayed with pesticides.

BLACKBERRY AND APPLE CRUMBLE Serves 8-10

METHOD

Preheat the oven to 180°C/350°F/gas mark 4 and grease a 20-centimetre, round, ovenproof dish.

Peel, core and chop the apples into roughly 1-centimetre cubes. Then rinse the blackberries. Add the fruit to a large pan along with a tablespoon of water and a tablespoon of the sugar. Cook the fruit uncovered on a low heat for 5 minutes, stirring occasionally, until it has softened a little. Once done, add the rest of the sugar, the cinnamon, allspice and salt. Stir thoroughly to combine and put to one side.

Meanwhile, put all the topping ingredients into a bowl and rub them together with the tips of your fingers until they resemble breadcrumbs. Alternatively, add all the ingredients to a food processor and pulse to achieve the same effect.

Put the fruit mixture into the bottom of the prepared dish, then sprinkle the crumble topping over the fruit evenly.

Bake for 30-40 minutes, until the fruit is bubbling and the top is golden brown. Allow to cool on a cooling rack before serving.

INGREDIENTS

For the topping:
200 g plain flour
150 g brown sugar
160 g butter
Pinch of salt

For the filling:
300 g cooking apples
150 g blackberries
60 g brown sugar
1 tbsp plain flour
1 tsp cinnamon
1 tsp allspice
½ tsp salt

STAY WILD

CONCLUSION

The great outdoors is the beating heart of our world, and it's vital for us to protect it and to cherish it. Hopefully, within these pages you will have found something to inspire you to reach out and explore this amazing source of life, energy and freedom. Whether you want to conquer the mountains, dive beneath the waves, discover fascinating wildlife, or simply bathe in the beauty of nature, every trip into the wild will be unique and an experience to treasure.

Over thousands of years, the natural world has shaped us and defined who we are, and maintaining a connection to it is something that we need not only to survive, but to thrive. If we give it the chance, the great outdoors can make our lives richer, more fulfilling and meaningful – all we need to do is take a step outside the front door...

THE EARTH
HAS ITS
MUSIC
FOR THOSE
WHO WILL
LISTEN.

GEORGE SANTAYANA

iMAGE CREDiTS

If you're interested in finding out more
about our books, find us on Facebook at
Summersdale Publishers and follow
us on Twitter at @Summersdale.

WWW.SUMMERSDALE.COM